Introducing Mental Health

Introducing Mental Health

A Practical Guide

Caroline Kinsella and Connor Kinsella

Foreword by Vikram Patel

Jessica Kingsley Publishers
London and Philadelphia

First published in 2006
by Jessica Kingsley Publishers
116 Pentonville Road
London N1 9JB, UK
and
400 Market Street, Suite 400
Philadelphia, PA 19106, USA

www.jkp.com

Library of Congress Cataloging in Publication Data
A CIP catalog record for this book is available from the Library of Congress

British Library Cataloguing in Publication Data
A CIP catalogue record for this book is available from the British Library

ISBN-13: 978 1 84310 260 1
ISBN-10: 1 84310 260 9

Printed and bound in Great Britain by
Printwise (Haverhill) Ltd, Suffolk

Dedicated to the memory of Suzanne Elaine West (1963–2005)

Acknowledgements

The authors would like to convey their gratitude to the many people who made this work possible. To our family and friends who have hardly seen us while we have been preparing and writing this book, and have kept us going with support, encouragement and even the odd chastisement. To the many people who have been on the receiving end of our efforts as both trainers and mental health professionals, and whose views and experiences form an invaluable core of this book. To the many inspirational people we have worked with over the years whose advice and wisdom has found its way into these pages, even if we did not appreciate it at the time. And special thanks to Aran and Ryan, who have had to put up with some very boring weekends!

Contents

Foreword

The World Health Organization estimates that about 400 million people worldwide suffer from a mental illness. If we include all types of mental disorders, about one in four people will suffer a mental disorder at some point in their lives. I don't need to be a psychiatrist to know that this figure is, if anything, an underestimate. Of the myriad varieties of mental illnesses that affect adults, some exact a more severe toll on the lives of the patient, and their families. Schizophrenia, bipolar disorder and major depressive disorders clearly stand out among these conditions for three reasons. First, because they are 'disorders', most closely approaching the illness paradigm of medicine. They begin at a certain point in a person's life, prior to which time the person was often functioning relatively well. When they do occur, though, their effect can be devastating. Thus, the second reason: these are the most crippling of all mental disorders. No wonder, then, that these three are among the leading mental disorders in the WHO league table of health problems causing disabilities. Third, because those with these disorders can be helped, through a judicious combination of medicines, psychological treatments and social interventions. We need no longer be nihilistic about the prognosis of people with mental disorders.

This book is clearly for a specific audience: those who are working in a caring profession with people with severe or chronic mental health problems, particularly people working in Britain. In Britain today, this may include a wide range of professionals, from nurses on a general medical ward to housing officers on a council estate, from social workers to placement workers helping people get back to work. Apart from the three conditions above, the book also deals with personality disorders (arguably the most difficult mental health problem to work with) and dual diagnosis, the situation when a person with a mental disorder also has a substance abuse problem. Not uncommon by any means and a complex clinical problem that needs sensitive and unique management skills. The content covers the aetiology and the clinical management of these disorders and manages to describe the significant advances in these areas, taking a balanced and sensible approach to the evidence and its implications.

What a pleasure to read a book about mental health where all the jargon has been stripped off leaving only the bare essentials. Essentials that not only capture the essence of mental health, and mental illness, but do so in a manner that makes one wonder why we need more complex psychiatric tomes at all!

Indeed, I imagine the book may be valuable not only for professionals but for persons with mental disorders and their families too; certainly, the way these authors have presented their material makes it eminently accessible for the community at large. What is really remarkable about this effort is the authors' ability to splice in humour liberally; it is not an easy task to integrate humour in a text on mental illness, while maintaining the highest standard of ethics and political correctness for people with mental illness. The style and layout is also innovative: they have used both handouts and summaries, the perfect tools for trainers, and so appropriate for our growing appetite for bite-sized information.

Caroline and Connor Kinsella's labour of love, surely borne out of many months (perhaps years) of gestation, is a perfect example of how health matters can be explained and shared in language that is clear and straightforward, without in any way diminishing the scientific basis of the material.

Vikram Patel, MRCPsych, PhD
London School of Hygiene and Tropical Medicine

Introduction: A Note from the Authors

Based on our many years' experience in both training and psychiatric practice, we have written this book with the aim of providing a clear and accessible guide to working with mentally disordered people. The text is designed with two main purposes in mind. First, as an immediately accessible reference for front-line professionals who need a good understanding of mental health issues, and second, as a training resource for those facilitating courses with such groups, with the inclusion of sections that can be copied onto overhead projector slides and used as handouts.

We have tried to focus on the needs of that increasingly large group of workers who offer care and support to a wide range of mentally disordered and vulnerable people, but have limited professional training or qualifications to complement their 'day-to-day' experience. Health care teams, social services, supported housing providers and other non-statutory agencies will all find this book a valuable resource, particularly when faced with situations and problems that have often proved difficult or even impossible to manage, and sometimes leave even the most resourceful and optimistic workers feeling dispirited and 'de-skilled'.

Divided into subject headings that focus on areas particularly relevant to this staff group, the text and related training materials contain clear outlines of some of the major issues and situations workers will encounter, together with key principles and simple techniques that can be used to help a wide variety of clients who at times present us with complex and problematic scenarios. We have also tried to make sense of the most frequently encountered psychiatric terminologies (in other words, the 'jargon') and explode some of the many myths that abound in this field.

With literally dozens of different diagnoses and a highly complicated arrangement of symptoms, behaviours and personality traits, which staff will come across on a daily basis, we have drawn on our experience in training hundreds of workers from a wide range of organizations and strived to maintain as narrow and relevant a focus as possible. The scope of the book is therefore limited to those mental health problems we believe to be most likely to render clients vulnerable and in need of long-term care and support. Schizophrenia, bipolar disorder and depression are discussed in some depth, along with chapters on personality disorder, self-harm and dual diagnosis.

Using this book

Readers will be aware of the range of terms used to describe the recipients of our services. 'Tenants', 'residents', 'patients', 'clients' or 'service users' are all in common use, but we have limited our terminology to 'clients' and 'patients' as and when necessary.

Each chapter looks at a particular area of interest and is divided into sections that define terms, outline key concepts and offer key skills and techniques to help readers address some of the most common problems encountered in day-to-day work.

The Handouts at the end of each chapter offer supplementary reading to complement the main text, while the 'Case notes' provide realistic descriptions of people and situations to help readers apply the factual material to familiar scenarios in the real world.

At the end of each chapter, trainers will also find bulleted summaries of the subjects covered in the chapter, which can also be copied and used as handouts or overhead projector (OHP) slides.

Further reading and research can be carried out with the help of the references and useful resources lists provided at the end of each chapter.

Chapter 1

Severe Mental Illness

Newspapers, magazines, radio, television documentaries and soap operas all regularly feature mental disorder as a theme. But despite the media exposure and the tireless promotion of major charities and awareness-raising bodies, mental health issues continue to be widely misunderstood, mythologized and stereotyped.

Terms such as 'loony', 'nutter' or 'a can short of a six-pack' are used to describe just about anyone who has, or may have, some form of mental health problem, often without any true conception of what these problems might be and how they might affect the sufferer. A common misconception is that mental disorders are permanent, serious, and almost always lead to hospital admission or 'being sectioned'.

In fact, defining what is (or what is not) a mental health problem is really a matter of degree. Nobody could be described as having 'good' mental health every minute of every day. Any football supporter will report the highs and lows encountered on an average Saturday afternoon, and can easily remember the euphoria of an important win or the despondency felt when their team is thrashed six-nil on a cold, wet Tuesday evening. But this could hardly be described as a 'mental health problem', and for all but the most ardent supporters their mood will have lifted within a short space of time.

However, the same person faced with redundancy, illness or the loss of a close family member might encounter something more akin to a 'problem'. They may experience, for example, anger, low mood, tearfulness, sleep difficulties and loss of appetite. This is a quite normal reaction to stressful life events, although the nature and degree of reaction is of course dependent on a number of factors such as the individual's personality, the circumstances of the loss and the support available from those around them at the time. In most circumstances the bereaved person will recover after a period of time and will return to a normal way of life without the need for medical intervention of any kind.

On the other hand, many people will experience mental health problems serious enough to warrant a visit to their general practitioner (GP). Statistics vary as to the exact proportion of the population who might experience mental health problems. It is commonly accepted that between one in four (Goldberg and Huxley 1992) and one in six adults (Singleton *et al.* 2000) will be experiencing significant mental health problems at any one time, although these figures vary according to what is defined as a 'problem' (see Handout 1.1 Measuring mental health).

The majority of people with mental health problems are successfully assessed and treated by GPs, practice nurses and practice counsellors, and will normally be able to carry on a reasonably normal lifestyle either during treatment or following a period of recovery. A small proportion of mental health problems seen by a GP will necessitate referral to a community mental health team (CMHT) for specialist assessment. Only a very small proportion will result in in-patient admission.

Nonetheless, there remains a sizeable group of individuals who suffer from severely debilitating disorders that drastically reduce their quality of life and may necessitate long-term support from family, carers, social services staff, not-for-profit agencies and charities, not to mention the mental health care professionals.

Mental health problems can be broadly divided into one of two groups: mental illness or mental disorder (see Handout 1.2 Illness or disorder?). This chapter aims to identify and describe the most well-known and debilitating mental illnesses, and clear up some of the misunderstanding that surrounds terms such as schizophrenia, bipolar disorder and depression.

Schizophrenia

This is a widely misunderstood term commonly referred to as meaning 'split personality'. In fact, the term 'schizophrenic' is increasingly and quite wrongly used by the media as an adjective to indicate a person or group who have two contrasting sides. To varying degrees schizophrenia means not a 'splitting' but a destruction of the personality, and is a potentially severe and debilitating psychotic illness (see Handout 1.3 Psychosis) if not diagnosed and treated as quickly as possible.

People with schizophrenia usually have more difficulty than most forming and maintaining relationships. They may also have difficulty working, and generally going about the day-to-day aspects of life most of us take for granted, such as driving a car or renting a flat. While modern drug treatments are often highly effective and relatively free of the serious side-effects of the older anti-psychotic treatments, schizophrenia more often than not requires high levels of support and social care from families, mental health professionals and social care agencies.

This is not to say that every person who suffers from schizophrenia is severely disabled. Contrary to popular wisdom among both the public and some mental health professionals, many schizophrenics are able to lead perfectly enjoyable, normal and often creative lives, particularly with appropriate social and professional support. The advent of modern anti-psychotic medications, which are much less likely to cause the sedating and disabling side-effects of their predecessors, has also done much to promote optimism for the future care of people with schizophrenia.

Schizophrenia can be experienced as a 'one off' episode with a full recovery, particularly with increased recognition and early intervention. However, with a worldwide incidence of 1 per cent of the general population, there remain many thousands of people in the UK with a lifelong, enduring illness, which, while adequately controlled with medical treatment and social support, may ebb and flow in severity, and will have a quite profound impact on that person's life and those around them.

Signs and symptoms

As a powerful and often misunderstood label, great care is taken by psychiatrists before diagnosing an individual as having schizophrenia. While each individual and situation is different, a diagnosis will depend on the presence of well-defined features or symptoms. As well as getting to know the person themselves, a psychiatrist will also wish to hear from family members, friends or anyone who has known the person well, particularly if they have known them 'pre-morbidly' or, in other words, before symptoms have begun to emerge.

Schizophrenia usually emerges in the late teens or early twenties in males, with women more typically becoming unwell later in life. The illness itself is usually preceded by a shy, quiet childhood and adolescence. Schizophrenics seldom have a wide network of friends and acquaintances prior to symptoms emerging, and may have been previously described by parents and teachers as isolated and withdrawn compared with their peers. Social withdrawal is often accentuated in the early stages of schizophrenia, with families often concerned that their son or daughter has locked themselves away in a bedroom, becoming disconnected from the outside world and behaving oddly.

The symptoms of schizophrenia are identified as belonging to one of two groups: positive or negative. Positive symptoms are more immediately obvious and are those features that are most likely to be identified by non-professionals as indicating that a person is seriously unwell.

POSITIVE SYMPTOMS

Loss of insight. As with other forms of psychotic illness, people diagnosed with schizophrenia usually lose insight into their situation. In other words they have little or no conception of being unwell. While mental health professionals, families and carers may clearly see a deterioration in a person's functioning and general well-being, sufferers themselves are oblivious to their situation and may take great exception to assessments, interviews and the attentions of mental health professionals. Loss of insight is a particularly disturbing aspect of schizophrenia. When a person has flu, appendicitis or even depression, they are almost always aware that they are unwell. Schizophrenia severely disrupts a person's understanding and perception of the real world, and the distressing experiences of schizophrenia are all too real to the sufferers themselves.

Delusions. Other indicators of schizophrenia include the presence of delusions. These are beliefs that are bizarre, at odds with a person's cultural experience, and cannot be proved objectively to be true. The person may describe being watched, for example, by hidden cameras or microphones. They may believe that the television or radio is communicating directly with them, or that their thoughts are being broadcast to others and are no longer private.

Medical reports may refer to 'passivity phenomena' or 'control experiences', meaning that the sufferer feels their thoughts and actions are controlled by a third party such as a real or imaginary character in that person's life, or by aliens, the church, the CIA or a political party.

Hallucinations. A further diagnostic indicator looked for by psychiatrists is the presence of hallucinations. A hallucination is a sensory perception that appears real only to the person experiencing that stimulus and can involve any of the senses. People suffering from epilepsy or brain injury sometimes experience olfactory (to do with the sense of smell) or visual hallucinations, but the most frequently described experiences in schizophrenia are the auditory hallucinations or 'voices' heard by them but inaudible to anyone else. Experiences such as these are sometimes associated with other illnesses and disorders, and are sometimes described by otherwise 'normal' people who have occasionally been misdiagnosed and treated on the basis of their voices.

Schizophrenics may, for example, hear the voice of one or more people giving them instructions, insulting them or even telling jokes. The so-called 'command hallucinations' are, as the name suggests, voices that direct the individual to carry out certain tasks or react in a particular way. For example, a sufferer's voices may command them to carry out seemingly bizarre rituals, or to keep the presence and identity of the voices secret, or even to harm themselves or others. This sometimes creates conflict in the mind of the person experiencing the commands and appears to those around them as a bizarre and heated argument with 'themselves'. The hearing of voices is frequently described as among the most upsetting and disorientating of symptoms, particularly when sufferers are forced to resist commands that they know are destructive or anti-social, or that those around them are unable to comprehend.

Thought disorder. This is another key indicator of schizophrenia, and can take the form of 'thought blocking' (not being able to think logically), 'thought insertion' (believing someone is putting thoughts into one's head) and 'thought broadcasting' (believing other people can hear one's thoughts).

The sufferer is unable to think in a logical progression, and thoughts and ideas may be heavily influenced and further confused by delusional ideas and hallucinations as described above. To the outside world this is most likely to become evident in a person's pattern of speech, which becomes erratic and confused. A thought disordered person's conversation appears jumbled as the individual jumps from topic to topic with little or no coherent pattern. Communication with the sufferer may become difficult if not impossible. Skilled and experienced mental health workers will know that simplicity is the key, and will attempt a very narrow focus of conversation in order to maintain at least some communication and rapport with the thought disordered person.

NEGATIVE SYMPTOMS

The phenomena described above are usually acute, or in other words are quite obvious and have an immediate impact on both the individual and those around them. However, with the appropriate identification and intervention, positive symptoms can be relatively short-lived. However, schizophrenia is also characterized by another set of features known as 'negative' symptoms, which are less obvious, more insidious and often present greater challenges to carers and mental health professionals. Social withdrawal, apathy, and an inability to concentrate for long periods of time are very common features of schizophrenia, which often persist long after more acute, positive symptoms have disappeared.

While it is certainly true that some of the features described here may be the result of prolonged treatment with powerful anti-psychotic drugs, negative symptoms exist even in those schizophrenics who have remained untreated with medication. In fact, as we shall see later in this chapter, modern 'atypical' anti-psychotic drugs are relatively free of the sedative effects of the older 'typical' anti-psychotic drugs and are designed to treat both positive and negative symptoms, the latter usually proving more difficult to treat than the more evident phenomena.

Medication aside, the carer's response to apathy, social isolation and poor or non-existent self-care is typically one of trying to look beyond the disappointment of watching the social decline of patients, clients or family members even when the more distressing features of the illness have subsided. A person may remain in bed all day, or sit in front of a television, or refuse all interaction with others, or refuse to wash, shower or change their clothes for weeks at a time.

There are certainly many fine examples of mental health rehabilitation offering much more in the way of 'normalization' and motivation than medication alone, but the degree to which carers or services intervene ultimately depends on the severity of the illness, the individual circumstances and the resources available to provide the energy, commitment and enthusiasm necessary to counter the devastating effects of schizophrenia in all its various manifestations.

What causes schizophrenia?

While there can be little doubt that certain illnesses such as lung cancer are closely linked with a 'causative factor' such as smoking, current research indicates that there is no clear cause of schizophrenia. Nonetheless, several factors are now well known to be associated with the illness, although the exact interaction remains under intense study and is likely to be highly complex. It is now well known that schizophrenia is associated with both chemical and structural brain dysfunction, although researchers are still very far from determining how these factors interlink, and how brain processes interact with important findings in genetics, and environmental processes such as early childhood development and upbringing.

THE BRAIN

Most research into the causes of schizophrenia has centred on dissection of the brains of deceased schizophrenia sufferers, although modern imaging and scanning techniques have allowed increasingly sophisticated views of the brain 'in vivo'.

It has been acknowledged for some time that the chemical dopamine is a key component in schizophrenia (Stahl 2000, p.374). Dopamine is a chemical messenger or 'neurotransmitter' associated with functions as diverse as movement and coordination, intellectual functioning and the experience of pleasure (see Handout 1.7 Neurotransmitters). The movement disorder Parkinson's Disease is related to abnormally low levels of dopamine, while recreational drugs such as cannabis, ecstasy and amphetamines cause over-production of dopamine along with another important neurotransmitter, serotonin. Some of the symptoms of schizophrenia, particularly the more acute 'positive' symptoms, appear to be related to over-production of dopamine. Traditional anti-psychotic drugs block the receptors in the brain that respond to dopamine, although other theories have suggested the importance of serotonin, another neurotransmitter that is also important in understanding mood disorders such as depression (Meltzer 1995). Serotonin and dopamine pathways are now thought to interact with one another, and while the exact mechanics of this interaction are as yet unknown, the more recent anti-psychotic medications (known as 'atypical anti-psychotics') affect levels of both these neurotransmitters in a way that causes less debilitating side-effects while addressing a wider range of both positive and negative symptoms.

In addition to studying the complexities of brain chemistry and its association with schizophrenia, researchers have been using sophisticated scanning equipment to look at the structural changes in the brains of schizophrenics. While several studies have detected abnormal brain structures and changes in the blood flow related to certain symptoms (Flashman and Green 2004), it has been known for some time that schizophrenia sufferers tend to have abnormally large ventricles (fluid-filled cavities in the brain) (Johnstone *et al.* 1976), although even these changes are not a reliable indicator of schizophrenia per se. One particularly problematic factor for brain researchers is the fact that regular brain activity in one area (memory, for example) has been found to affect the size and shape of parts of the brain over time (Maguire *et al.* 2000). In other words, repetitive memory tests may increase the size of that part of the brain responsible for recall. It is therefore difficult to determine whether structural changes in the schizophrenic brain are the cause of symptoms such as hallucinations or delusional thoughts, or have been caused by the symptoms themselves.

HEREDITY

There is certainly little doubt that schizophrenia along with other psychotic disorders such as bipolar disorder are hereditary to some degree. However, we are still some way from describing schizophrenia as a genetic illness in a similar way to Huntingdon's Chorea or sickle cell anaemia, where carriers of faulty genes can be readily identified through blood tests and prospective parents can be offered counselling to outline the relative risks of transmitting a disease to their children. The standard probability of developing schizophrenia is a constant 1 per cent worldwide, although this probability increases markedly where a child's parents or close relatives have a history of schizophrenia. Despite occasional media reports of the discovery of a 'schizophrenia gene', the exact whereabouts of the switch in a person's genotype, which turns on or off the symptoms of schizophrenia, remains elusive. The picture is further clouded by the inability of genetics to accurately predict an individual's propensity to develop the illness.

While genetic factors are an undoubtedly important area of further research into the causes of schizophrenia, the role of heredity does not offer a simple cause-and-effect relationship and our knowledge in this area has been complicated both by problems of definition (of schizophrenia) and by 'confounding factors' such as the environment in which a child has been brought up. Not all 'high risk' children develop schizophrenia in adulthood, and some develop the illness with no family history whatsoever, but recent advances in relating individual genes to specific brain abnormalities are leading the way toward a more subtle and much greater understanding of how a person with schizophrenia develops schizophrenia (Owen, O'Donovan and Harrison 2005).

THE ENVIRONMENT

In the 1960s and early 1970s, the 'anti-psychiatry' movement postulated that schizophrenia was the manifestation of illness within the family unit as a whole, although only one family member presented with symptoms (see Handout 1.4 The anti-psychiatry movement).

According to the anti-psychiatry movement, schizophrenia was thought to be a psychological and social phenomenon that had little to do with altered brain structure or chemistry, and benefited little from powerful drugs that merely dimmed the patient's personality without addressing the true dysfunction within the family as a whole. While this movement enjoyed many years of popularity among both mental health professionals and those opposed to what they saw as the 'medicalization' of mental health, the theories have led to some ground-breaking research into the role of the family and carers in schizophrenia, which in turn has left us with the important concept of 'expressed emotion' (Kuipers and Raune 1999).

While researchers have yet to find clear developmental factors that might cause schizophrenia, family members (and more recently, carers, whether professional or otherwise) have been consistently found to belong to one of two broad groups: those that have high expressed emotion (HEE) or low expressed emotion (LEE). The former tend to become over-involved with the schizophrenia sufferer, attempting to force them into activities or socialization. This may also manifest as irritation and hostility, particularly where the subject of their attention is unwilling to cooperate, or responds with increasingly bizarre behaviours and conversation. The LEE carers are more relaxed in their attitudes and will make more allowances for the illness both in terms of positive and negative symptoms. Based on the results of numerous valid and reliable research findings, mental health professionals are now trained to deliver psychosocial interventions that enable HEE families and carers to lower their levels of expressed emotion, the result being that relapses decrease markedly and overall social functioning generally improves (Marshall and Lockwood 2003).

Bipolar disorder

Perhaps better known as manic depression, bipolar disorder is a severe mental illness, which, like schizophrenia, belongs to the psychosis group of disorders. With an incidence of approximately 1 per cent of the population it is as common as schizophrenia, and although it shares many of the features of the latter, there are a number of key differences.

The person with bipolar disorder usually experiences lengthy periods of emotional and social stability interspersed with episodes of severe low mood or extreme excitement and overactivity. The popular view of bipolar disorder is that these two states alternate neatly with one another, although the real picture is often more complex than this, with one mood state being experienced more frequently and more severely than the other. As there are several variants of the illness with different patterns of low mood and overactivity, some mental health professionals refer to bipolar spectrum disorder, bipolar affective disorder ('affect' meaning 'mood') or bipolar I and bipolar II.

The severity of the condition varies widely from person to person. Some sufferers may experience only occasional extremes of mood during a lifetime, especially if they are taking mood stabilizing medication and are well supported by both family and professional care staff. In these circumstances bipolar disorder does not appear to create the same degree of social withdrawal and debilitation as schizophrenia. In other words, people with bipolar disorder often manage to live otherwise normal lives with careers, families and mortgages to pay.

On the other hand, the 'rapid cycling' form of bipolar disorder, where extremes of mood are experienced more than four times within a year, may leave the sufferer disabled by altered moods and psychotic symptoms for much of their adult life and cause significant lifestyle disruption. Severity of symptoms and rapid cycling have been associated with cognitive impairment (a reduced ability to think, reason and solve problems) and social disability whereby the sufferer faces great difficulties in forming and maintaining relationships, finding employment or enjoying many of the lifestyle norms most of us take for granted.

Bipolar disorder typically manifests between the late teens and mid-twenties, and like schizophrenia tends to develop earlier in men than women. However, clear diagnosis may take considerable time and it is not unusual for sufferers to describe intervals of many years between first symptoms and a diagnosis being made.

Both the 'highs' and 'lows' of bipolar disorder share many features with other 'standalone' conditions such as schizophrenia or depression. When a person experiences one or other of these states at different times, sometimes separated by months or even years and not necessarily following the neat pattern usually attributed to this illness, psychiatrists need to be very clear about a diagnosis before they and other professionals would want to tell the patient they are suffering from a severe and enduring mental illness that can be controlled but not cured, and will most likely affect them for the rest of their lives.

While the profile of 'highs' and 'lows' or 'mania' and 'depression' may be somewhat simplistic, this broad picture of bipolar disorder is reasonably descriptive and the next section will take a closer look at what these terms mean in practice.

Mania: the 'highs'

Carers, families and sufferers may often hear references to either 'mania' or 'hypomania', and while students of psychiatry may be required to carefully define either condition, in practice the presentations are indistinguishable from one another. In effect, a manic episode has the potential for very serious repercussions, and left untreated may result in catastrophe and in some cases serious injury or death, which was often the case prior to the discovery of effective drug treatments in the middle of the last century. Superficially at least, the person experiencing this stage of the illness may appear elated, happy and full of energy and ideas, but either manic or depressive phases of bipolar disorder are often 'triggered' by stress or untoward life events such as bereavement or redundancy. In fact, in some cultures, mania is an expression of extreme sadness or distress as opposed to the low mood and lack of motivation more often seen in the West.

Initially the manic phase may present as little more than insomnia and restlessness. For those who have experienced manic episodes before this is often a key 'early warning sign' (see Handout 1.5 Early warning signs) and seeking help at this stage may prevent further progression to the complete chaos of full-blown mania.

People with experience of bipolar disorder often refer to the dilemma of entering the manic phase (Adams 2002). At this stage individuals remain aware of what is happening and that they are becoming unwell. However, the need to seek intervention, which will usually involve some form of tranquillizing medication, is compromised by the feelings of elation and the intense creativity that accompany this phase. People with a history of bipolar disorder often enthuse about the highly pleasurable aspect of mania, particularly prior to the descent into full-scale, insightless chaos. They describe feelings of intense creativity and can sometimes produce evidence of this as can dozens of famous bipolar poets, artists and novelists throughout the last century. People who have experienced mania can recall intense feelings of pleasure and 'oneness' with others, and describe with some enthusiasm the omnipotence and greatly enhanced self-esteem that is often at odds with their usual personality. Even with the benefit of hindsight, those with a history of bipolar disorder and manic phases in particular are often torn between the lure of a wonderful few days of elation and excitement, and the knowledge that early mania is but 'the calm before the storm', and that steps need to be taken before the situation becomes catastrophic.

As mania progresses, speech becomes rapid and increasingly disorganized, jumping from topic to topic in no particular order. Two-way conversation becomes difficult if not impossible as the person appears desperate to communicate their ideas, which by this stage are appearing faster than they can talk, leading to even more rapid speech and an increase in volume. By this time extreme restlessness may have become apparent and the individual may have lost insight into their situation, crossing the boundary between the real world and their psychotic experience of extreme power, creativity and energy. Delusional beliefs of superiority, wealth and omnipotence may have surfaced by this stage. Credit card companies are constantly dealing with situations where people with bipolar disorder have spent hundreds or even thousands of pounds on shopping sprees, cars or donations to charities while unwell. If left untreated and unsupported by families or carers, manic people may become highly vulnerable to exploitation and are easily distracted or lured into financial scams or sexual promiscuity.

Behaviour becomes increasingly bizarre, often involving uncharacteristically loud clothing, extreme restlessness (running rather than walking) and public displays that may draw the attentions of police. Mania is often characterized as 'elation' and the opposite extreme of depression, although irritability and aggression are not uncommon, particularly where the person's ideas are contradicted or their extremes of behaviour are curtailed.

As with schizophrenia, delusional ideas are expressed, often involving grandiose self-images of world domination/salvation/genius/omnipotence etc. Where insight has disappeared, attempts by carers, families or health care staff to contradict numerous and sometimes bizarre ideas and theories are unlikely to be helpful. The manic person's theory that they are 'working on a machine that will bring about world peace' may appear absurd to anyone else, but contradiction will be invariably met with disbelief, frustration and sometimes anger. By this stage, and without medical intervention and support, which may involve hospital admission, the sufferer may not have slept for several nights and, in the absence of any interest in food or drink, may have become malnourished and dehydrated.

Fortunately, modern methods of recognition and early intervention have prevented much of the chaos and embarrassment caused by mania, although living with the consequences of wild overspending and bizarre behaviour remains one of the key problems for sufferers of bipolar disorder. Sufferers often liken the 'come down' from mania as akin to the morning after a party, having to face the consequences of a drunken night of arguing, insults and outrageous behaviour eagerly reported by friends but scarcely remembered by the protagonists themselves.

Depression: the 'lows'

Clinical depression is perhaps the most common and widespread of the mental disorders, and is a mental illness in its own right, sometimes referred by mental health professionals as 'unipolar depression' to distinguish it from the type of depression that alternates with mania.

In terms of bipolar disorder, the feelings of intense low mood, fatigue and lack of motivation associated with depression represent the polar opposite of mania. Of course, 'depression' (with a small 'd') has a meaning and context in the English language that suggests sadness and misery, but fails to convey the psychiatric context and its potential severity as a long-term, persistent mental illness. We shall be taking a more detailed look at depression later in this chapter, but for the time being let us take a brief look at this condition in the context of bipolar disorder.

Whereas unipolar depression develops gradually over a period of weeks or even months, the onset of depression in bipolar disorder tends to have a more sudden and dramatic onset, in some cases immediately following a manic phase.

There is also a tendency toward greater severity of symptoms. At its most serious, depression has the potential to leave an individual mute and immobile, unable to communicate or carry out even basic tasks such as washing, dressing or eating. While psychotic symptoms such as loss of insight, hallucinations and delusional ideas are occasionally a feature of unipolar depression, they are more likely to occur as part of bipolar disorder, and often take the form of paranoia and derogatory voices as opposed to the grandiose and bizarre ideas a person may express during mania. The risk of suicide is always heightened by severe depression, particularly where the person is troubled by voices or delusional ideas, which in some cases may 'command' the individual into acts of self-harm or suicide.

Treatment may again be required within a safe hospital setting. In addition to the essential support of friends and family, those experiencing the depressive phase of bipolar disorder will normally be treated with anti-depressant medication. This is normally effective within two to three weeks and works by altering levels of serotonin in the brain. Normally prescribed on a long-term, preventative basis, the prescription of anti-depressants in bipolar disorder is a somewhat more delicate affair as there remains the risk of 'overshooting' the person's mood back into elation.

What causes bipolar disorder?

The latest research suggests that there is no single cause of bipolar disorder, but that several key factors interact with one another. Genetics, childhood development, life stress and brain biology all appear to have a significant role in the development of the illness (Craddock and Jones 2002). Current knowledge suggests the emergence of a model that encompasses both 'nurture' and 'nature' explanations, or put in other words, the environmental and the biological. It appears possible, if not probable, that an individual is born with a genetic predisposition to develop bipolar disorder. However, this predisposition is not confined to a single gene but a complex combination of inherited factors that is as yet undefined, and requires 'switching on' as the individual matures into adolescence or early adulthood.

While we are still many years away from being able to draw an accurate picture of how brain structure and biochemistry is implicated in causing bipolar disorder, there remains the possibility that brain abnormalities may be determined by genetic factors, although current research is unable to determine whether these abnormalities exist prior to the emergence of symptoms or have emerged subsequent to the development of the illness.

There is also evidence that a higher than expected number of sufferers have histories of childhood trauma and abuse (Garno et al. 2005). It is theorized that bipolar disorder is biologically determined to some extent, but may require a combination of 'trigger factors' such as extreme stress experienced by an individual who is psychologically and genetically vulnerable.

THE BRAIN

Brain structure and chemistry have been studied in some detail in recent years, particularly with the emergence of sophisticated imaging techniques such as positron emission tomography (PET) and magnetic resonance imaging (MRI) scanners (Strakowski *et al.* 1999). Nonetheless, several types of brain abnormality (particularly within the deeper, more 'primitive' parts of the brain) have been identified so far that, while not indicating that bipolar sufferers are 'brain damaged' as such, do provide intriguing suggestions as to the mechanics of the illness and how future treatments may target those areas of brain functioning directly linked to the psychotic symptoms and mood swings of bipolar disorder. The ability of cutting-edge scanning techniques to study the brain in detail while certain tasks are completed or emotions experienced has enabled scientists to see a far more detailed picture of what is happening inside the brains of mentally ill individuals. Extreme mood states can now be linked with different structures and processes within the brain, and researchers are beginning to identify possible differences in the way that the bipolar disorder brain processes emotions and stimuli compared with the 'normal' brain.

People experiencing manic and/or psychotic symptoms are usually prescribed the same anti-psychotic drugs used to treat schizophrenia. Most of these drugs work by blocking off the brain's dopamine receptors, and as with schizophrenia, an over-abundance of the neurotransmitter dopamine appears to play a key role. Studies using PET scans (which offer a 'live' image of the brain in action using radioactive isotopes given to the patient prior to scanning) suggest that some people with bipolar disorder have an increased density of dopamine receptor cells in their brains compared with normal subjects, or those with bipolar disorder that does not result in psychotic symptoms.

As a final note on the biology of bipolar disorder, it is important to stress that the studies outlined above remain speculative at this stage and, while undoubtedly exciting, are subject to a number of restraints (such as the fluctuating and highly volatile nature of the subject area) and have yet to be subject to the checks and balances that separate scientific fact from mere hypothesis.

While research into biological factors such as genetics and brain function are undoubtedly leading toward a greater understanding of the causes of bipolar disorder, the fact remains that not everyone with the genetic or biological risk factors develops the illness, and some people who do suffer from the illness have no family history at all.

HEREDITY

First, there is evidence of a significant genetic link (Jones, Hayward and Lam 2002). Close relatives of people with bipolar disorder are much more likely to have the illness themselves, a fact already well known to mental health workers who are accustomed to parents and children sharing a history of bipolar disorder. Nonetheless, children of bipolar parents do not always develop the illness, and studies of identical twins reveal that while one twin may become ill, the same is not necessarily the case for the other. As identical twins are genetically identical, this alone is powerful evidence that bipolar disorder is not entirely dependent on one or more genes. For bipolar disorder to emerge, the evidence suggests that while an individual may have a genetic predisposition to the illness, other factors need to come into the equation before symptoms appear.

THE ENVIRONMENT

This points toward the study of a sufferer's environment, both in terms of the past and the 'here and now'. It has been known for some time that life stress often precipitates both the initial emergence of bipolar symptoms, and subsequent episodes of either mania or depression. Bereavement, starting university, a failed relationship or exam stress are all examples of events that can trigger a first emergence of bipolar symptoms, and subsequent relapses are often precipitated by problems at work or home.

A recent study has also found as many as 50 per cent of bipolar disorder patients reported histories of childhood abuse and trauma, and that such individuals were more likely to experience more severe symptoms and suffer from 'rapid cycling' as described earlier (Garno *et al.* 2005).

Other theories suggest that people with bipolar disorder have been subject to criticism or have been over-protected by their parents during childhood, and that the violent extremes of mood represent a lack of self-esteem and an inability to contain strong emotions. This theory certainly has parallels to the robust and widely accepted 'expressed emotion' theory applied to the treatment of schizophrenia, although this hypothesis remains an anecdotal rather than an evidence-based theory and has yet to be tested in clinical research (Honig *et al.* 1997).

Depression

Everyone experiences feelings of low mood and despondency at some stage in their lives, but depression can be described as an 'illness' when feelings of despair, along with an inability to carry out normal day-to-day life, becomes so prolonged and severe that medical intervention is required. Professionals often refer to this as 'clinical' depression. It may affect a person as a 'one off' event, recur at intervals throughout a person's life, or continue to affect the sufferer as a 'chronic' illness over a period of many years. While a diagnosis is made on the basis of several key symptoms, clinical depression can vary widely in both intensity and the way that it is experienced by the individual and those around them. For this reason it is difficult to simply list the signs and symptoms of depression, but we shall outline how this illness might appear in different forms and levels of severity.

At its most serious and debilitating, depression may lead to an inability to move, communicate, or carry out even basic tasks such as eating and drinking. Mental health professionals often refer to this state as 'physical retardation'. In this instance, serious physical illness and even death are immediate potential hazards and hospital admission may prove essential as will treatment with anti-depressants or, in emergency situations, electroconvulsive therapy (ECT) (see Handout 1.6 Electroconvulsive therapy (ECT)). The person will also need assistance with nutrition, hydration and basic self-care tasks.

Less severe episodes of depression are more common but may nonetheless leave the sufferer incapable of most everyday tasks and frightened of meeting others. They may be unwilling to leave the house or even get out of bed without considerable effort, and suicidal thoughts are not uncommon. Medical assessment and intervention in such cases is almost always required, with an assessment of suicide risk forming a key determinant of whether the person will require more intrusive interventions such as hospital admission or close monitoring at home by relatives and mental health professionals.

While the scenarios outlined above represent emergency situations with high risks of harm to the individual concerned, complete recovery is possible, particularly with the benefit of ongoing drug treatments and 'talking therapies' such as those described later in this chapter.

Alternatively, depression may sometimes be experienced as an ongoing, or 'chronic', condition that can nonetheless be tolerated and managed to the extent that a person is able to carry on a reasonably normal lifestyle including work and family responsibilities. However, they may not enjoy life to the same extent as most people and may experience a negative, pessimistic outlook on life. Stress or upsetting life events may prove more difficult than for most people and may prompt more severe symptoms such as loss of appetite, sleep disturbance or suicidal thoughts.

Whatever the severity or impact of illness on the person's life, depression sufferers cannot simply 'snap out of it'. They will need the ongoing support of family, friends and health professionals alongside appropriate drug treatments and psychological therapies. If depression is a recurring problem, onset will usually be relatively gradual and 'early warning signs' (see Handout 1.5 Early warning signs) can be identified to prompt immediate action, which may prevent further deterioration or slow down the progress of the more debilitating symptoms.

A diagnosis of depression will usually be made on the basis of a patient's self-report, but information from a friend or relative may prove invaluable, particularly in situations where the person has difficulty expressing their feelings or is unable to communicate at all. Persistent low mood is obviously a key diagnostic factor, but other symptoms such as sleep disturbance, loss of appetite or loss of interest in normally enjoyable activities will often be noted, along with a general feeling of hopelessness and very low self-esteem. A depressed person often experiences intrusive, negative thoughts, with constant rumination over past events, current problems or perceived disasters yet to come. They may voice beliefs such as 'What is the point of living?' or 'Everyone hates me, including me!', which will not respond to any amount of reassurance from those around them.

Tiredness and fatigue are almost always associated with depression, although it is not uncommon for people to throw themselves into work or other activities in a usually vain attempt to 'shrug off' their feelings or divert themselves from constant negative thoughts.

Substance misuse and dependence have a close relationship with depression, with heavy drinkers and drug users being more likely to be clinically depressed than the general population (Weaver *et al.* 2002). However, the relationship represents something of a 'chicken or egg' situation and it is important for mental health professionals to determine whether heavy substance use precedes depression or is an attempt by the already depressed person to mask symptoms, blot out feelings or 'self-medicate'.

As mentioned above, some individuals are unable to verbally articulate their feelings. Whether this is due to learning disability, the language barrier or the 'retardation' caused by depression itself, carers can still identify this condition by awareness of the features outlined above and discuss with a GP or mental health professional to avoid either a first episode or any deterioration of an existing depressive illness. A significant number of depressed GP attenders are only identified as suffering from depression through reports of physical health problems (MacHale 2002).

Furthermore, many languages have no equivalent of 'depression' as it is understood in English. Health professionals working with ethnic minority communities will be well aware that a number of people will experience depression as 'somatic' or physical health problems such as recurrent headaches, stomach pains or flu-like symptoms (Patel 2001).

What causes depression?

At the risk of sounding repetitive, no single cause of depression has yet been identified, although the neurotransmitters serotonin, noradrenaline and dopamine (see Handout 1.7 Neurotransmitters) lie at the heart of biological explanations of depression.

It is well known that some sufferers only experience symptoms between the months of September and April each year. Seasonal affective disorder (SAD) is a form of depression triggered by the comparative absence of natural light during the autumn and winter months. Natural light has a powerful effect on mood and reacts with biochemical agents and brain processes to regulate mood, with certain people being particularly sensitive to the relative darkness of autumn and winter. Fortunately for SAD sufferers the treatment of this condition is, in psychiatric terms, relatively simple. Light boxes are available that can be placed on a desk and mimic the effect of daylight, thus restoring biological balance and restoring the sufferer's mood, often without the need for anti-depressants. Unfortunately, other variants of depression are neither explained so simply nor treated so effectively without the need for drugs or psychological therapy. The cause of depression is as complex and varied as the manifestations of the illness itself, and appears to be a combination of genetic, biological and 'life event' factors.

First instances of depression, or relapses of an existing illness, are frequently preceded by stress, trauma, physical illness or bereavement. For example, unemployed people (particularly men) are much more likely to suffer depression than those with jobs, as are those with health conditions such as chronic pain or Parkinson's Disease (National Collaborating Centre for Mental Health 2004). While it may not come as any surprise that traumatic life events or difficult situations may precipitate depression, the exact mechanism of how external events impact upon a person's internal world to the extent that they may be rendered suicidal, mute or incapable of looking after themselves remains elusive.

References

Adams, B. (2002) *The Pits and the Pendulum: A Life with Bipolar Disorder.* London: Jessica Kingsley Publishers.

American Psychiatric Association (2000) *Diagnostic and Statistical Manual of Mental Disorders, Fourth Edition.* Washington, DC: American Psychiatric Association.

Craddock, N. and Jones, I. (2002) 'Molecular genetics of bipolar disorder.' *British Journal of Psychiatry 178*, 128–133.

de Girolamo, G. and Dotto, P. (2000) 'Epidemiology of personality disorders.' In M.G. Gelder, J.J. Lopez-Ibor and N.C. Andreasen (eds) *New Oxford Textbook of Psychiatry, vol. 1.* Oxford: Oxford University Press.

Fergusson, D., Doucette, S., Cranley Glass, K., Shapiro, S., Healy, D., Hebert, P. and Hutton, B. (2005) 'Association between suicide attempts and selective serotonin reuptake inhibitors: systematic review of randomized controlled trials.' *British Medical Journal 330*, 7488, 396.

Flashman, L. and Green, M. (2004) 'Review of cognition and brain structure in schizophrenia: profiles, longitudinal course, and effects of treatment.' *Psychiatric Clinics of North America 27*, 1, 1–18.

Garno, J., Goldberg, J., Ramirez, P. and Ritzler, B. (2005) 'Impact of childhood abuse on the clinical course of bipolar disorder.' *British Journal of Psychiatry 186*, 121–125.

Goldberg, D. and Huxley, P. (1992) *Common Mental Disorders: A Biosocial Model.* London: Routledge Press.

Honig, A., Hofman, A., Rozendaal, N. and Dingemans, P. (1997) 'Psycho-education in bipolar disorder: effect on expressed emotion.' *Psychiatry Research 72*, 1, 17–22.

Johnstone, E., Crow, T., Frith, C., Husband, J. and Kreel, L. (1976) 'Cerebral ventricular size and cognitive impairment in chronic schizophrenia.' *Lancet 2*, 7992, 924–926.

Jones, S., Hayward, P. and Lam, D. (2002) *Coping with Bipolar Disorder: A Guide to Living with Manic Depression.* Oxford: Oneworld Publications.

Kuipers, E. and Raune, D. (1999) 'The early development of expressed emotion and burden in the families of first onset psychosis.' In M. Birchwood and D. Fowler (eds) *Early Intervention in Psychosis.* London: Wiley.

Laing, R.D. (1960, 1990) *The Divided Self: An Existential Study in Sanity and Madness.* London: Penguin.

MacHale, S. (2002) 'Managing depression in physical illness.' *Advances in Psychiatric Treatment 8,* 297–304.

Maguire, E., Gadian, D., Johnsrude, I., Good, C., Ashburner, R., Frackowiak, S. and Frith, C. (2000) 'Navigation-related structural change in the hippocampi of taxi drivers.' *Proceedings of the National Academy of Sciences USA 9,* 8, 4398–4403.

Marazziti, D., Akiskal, H., Rossi, A. and Cassano, G. (1999) 'Alteration of the platelet serotonin transporter in romantic love.' *Psychological Medicine 29,* 3, 741–745.

Marshall, M. and Lockwood, A. (2003) *Early Intervention for People with Psychosis.* Leeds: NIMHE and Department of Health Policy Research Programme expert briefing.

Meltzer, H. (1995) 'The role of serotonin in schizophrenia and the place of serotonin-dopamine antagonist antipsychotics.' *Journal of Clinical Psychopharmacology 15,* 1, Suppl 1, 2S–3S.

National Collaborating Centre for Mental Health (2004) *Depression: Management of Depression in Primary and Secondary Care: Clinical Guideline 23.* London: National Institute for Clinical Excellence.

National Institute for Clinical Excellence (2003) *Guidance on the Use of Electroconvulsive Therapy: Technology Appraisal No. 59.* London: National Institute for Clinical Excellence.

Owen, M., O'Donovan, M. and Harrison, P. (2005) 'Schizophrenia: a genetic disorder of the synapse?' *British Medical Journal 330,* 158–159.

Patel, V. (2001) 'Cultural factors and international epidemiology.' *British Medical Bulletin 57,* 1, 33–45.

Singleton, N., Bumpstead, R., O'Brien, M., Lee, A. and Meltzer, H. (2000) *Psychiatric Morbidity Among Adults Living in Private Households in Great Britain.* London: Office for National Statistics.

Stahl, S.M. (2000) *Essential Psychopharmacology, Second Edition.* Cambridge: Cambridge University Press.

Strakowski, S.M., DelBello, M., Sax, K., Zimmerman, M., Hawkins, J.M., Shear, P. and Larson, E.R. (1999) 'Brain magnetic resonance imaging of structural abnormalities in bipolar disorder.' *Archives of General Psychiatry 56,* 3, 254–260.

Szasz, T. (1960, 1984) *Myth of Mental Illness: Foundations of a Theory of Personal Contact.* New York: Harper and Row.

Weaver, T., Charles, V., Madden, P. and Renton, A. (2002) *Co-morbidity of Substance Misuse and Mental Illness Collaborative Study: (COSMIC).* London: Department of Health.

World Health Organization (1992) *ICD-10: Classification of Mental and Behavioural Disorders.* Geneva: World Health Organization.

Useful resources

Websites

HyperGUIDE to the Mental Health Act: www.hyperguide.co.uk/mha

Institute of Psychiatry: www.iop.kcl.ac.uk

Mental Health Foundation: www.mentalhealth.org.uk

MIND: www.mind.org.uk

Rethink: www.rethink.org.uk

Revolving Doors: www.revolving-doors.co.uk

SANE: www.sane.org.uk

Books

Fernando, S. (1991) *Mental Health, Race and Culture.* London: Mind Publications.

Littlewood, R. and Lipsedge, M. (1982, 1998) *Aliens and Alienists.* London: Routledge.

Patel, V. (2003) *Where There is no Psychiatrist: A Mental Health Care Manual.* London: Gaskell Publications.

Pilgrim, D. and Rogers, A. (1998) *A Sociology of Mental Health and Illness.* Milton Keynes: Oxford University Press.

Prior, P. (1999) *Gender and Mental Health.* London: Macmillan.

Ryan, A. and Pritchard, J. (eds) (2004) *Good Practice in Adult Mental Health.* London: Jessica Kingsley Publishers.

Case notes: Elizabeth

Elizabeth is 26 and has been living in a housing association flat for two years. She is from rural Yorkshire, but came to London after leaving home after many arguments about her odd behaviour. She has stayed with other family members for short periods of time, but either walked out or was asked to leave. She occasionally booked into night shelters or hostels, but her habits led to disputes with other residents and she would invariably move on elsewhere.

Elizabeth insists on washing her hands 24 times after using the toilet, or before eating. This is a carefully prepared ritual and can take up to an hour. She has always been very guarded about her reasons for doing this, but has disclosed to mental health professionals that if she does not do this she will catch AIDS and die. Elizabeth also insists on changing her shoes 24 times in any one 24-hour period (fortunately she has several pairs) and recites the Lord's Prayer 24 times at midnight every night.

One night while sleeping rough in London, Elizabeth was approached by police and asked to leave a public toilet in a train station following a complaint from a member of the public. She became aggressive and threatening, screaming at the police officers that if she could not wash herself 24 times she would die, and she would kill anyone who tried to prevent her. She was arrested and taken to a psychiatric unit, and subsequently detained under the Mental Health Act for further assessment when she refused to stay voluntarily. Elizabeth was dirty and dishevelled, carrying her belongings (including an assortment of shoes) in two carrier bags. She was isolated and withdrawn, refusing to talk to staff or other patients, although it was noticed she appeared to be talking and laughing in her room even though nobody was with her at the time.

Following a period of further assessment, and several altercations with other patients over her ritualistic behaviour, Elizabeth began to confide in one of the medical staff. The doctor found Elizabeth difficult to understand, but listened carefully to what she was saying and was able to reflect back to her one or two statements that were constantly repeated, mainly around the significance of the number '24' and her 'spiritual guides' who guided her actions and demanded complete obedience, which would be punished by infection with AIDS if she did not comply. Having spent several sessions with Elizabeth the doctor had learnt the names of the three spiritual guides and discovered that they sometimes spoke to her when she was alone, and although they were sometimes funny and made her laugh, they were usually rude and threatening.

Elizabeth (continued)

The doctor empathized with Elizabeth, but suggested to her that her beliefs, and the voices of the spiritual guides, were probably the result of a severe mental illness that could be treated with medication. Elizabeth was initially resistive to this, and claimed that her voices had become even angrier with her for talking to a member of staff about them. However, she was eventually persuaded to try an anti-psychotic treatment, and was warned of possible side-effects and given a simple information sheet that explained how the drug worked.

Over the course of the next week, Elizabeth reported that the spiritual guides were becoming 'quieter' and she was not quite so afraid of them. She also became a little more communicative with others, although she still felt compelled to fulfil at least some of her rituals. She subsequently agreed to stay on the ward voluntarily and was taken off the section of the Mental Health Act. After several more weeks a care programme approach (CPA) meeting was convened on the unit where she was introduced to staff from a local housing association. Elizabeth had agreed that they come to discuss accommodation at a mental health after-care hostel, and a plan of care was agreed for her discharge in a fortnight's time. A community psychiatric nurse (CPN) was allocated to Elizabeth to act as her care coordinator after discharge.

In the meantime she visited the hostel and began to spend overnight stays there. After discharge from the psychiatric unit Elizabeth remained at the hostel for a further six months. During this time her hand-washing rituals and occasional truculence remained problematic for other residents and staff, and on several occasions she stopped taking medication and quickly became unwell again. However, her care coordinator arranged for Elizabeth to attend a local support group for people suffering with psychotic illness, where Elizabeth learnt more about schizophrenia and the medication she was prescribed. Although she constantly complained that the medication 'drained her strength' and made her feel hungry all the time, she gradually learnt how the medication acted on her brain to correct some of the processes that could make her seriously ill. Elizabeth also enrolled at college to take the GCSEs she had failed while at school.

After the first six months at the hostel, Elizabeth was offered a flat managed by the housing association. This allowed her to carry out her rituals without bothering anyone else, and although her care coordinator suggested that she might be happier without the compulsion to wash her hands, Elizabeth flatly refused any further help, saying that her 'spiritual guides' had never really gone away, but were 'just lying low for the time being'.

✓

Elizabeth (continued)

Elizabeth: points for reflection

1. What features can you identify that might suggest Elizabeth suffers from a mental illness?

2. What are her immediate needs prior to being admitted to hospital?

3. Why should Elizabeth require compulsory detention in hospital under the Mental Health Act?

4. Can you identify the most helpful aspects of Elizabeth's stay in hospital?

5. Can you identify the most helpful aspects of her after-care and support following discharge from hospital?

Case notes: Richard

Richard is usually a pleasant and gregarious character who keeps himself smart and tidy despite his unusual lifestyle. He can talk with some authority on literature and the arts, and is valued by other homeless people for his advice and help with completing forms and reading letters.

He was married for 13 years until the death of his wife from cancer. They had no children. Richard had run a successful printing business for many years prior to his wife's death, but found this increasingly difficult and sold it a year after his wife died. Within a very short period of time he had spent the proceeds of his business sale on a 'champagne' lifestyle of luxury cars, hotels and flights all over the world, and was eventually admitted to a psychiatric unit in France after running naked down the Champs-Elysées while singing 'Rule Britannia' through a megaphone.

He was transferred to a local unit, and settled quickly with medication, but attempted suicide shortly after being discharged and was readmitted. Richard left the hospital and disappeared. He sold his house and donated most of the money to various charities, placing a small amount in a trust fund from which he draws a weekly allowance. He has been living in various cities around the country, sleeping in his car and eating sandwiches and burgers.

Recently, Richard has become preoccupied with George Orwell's book *Down and Out in Paris and London* and is planning a return to Paris to live out his literary hero's life as a tramp. He has been discussing ways of drawing out all the remaining cash from his accounts and is hoping to hire a Santa Claus outfit and walk through the West End handing out £20 notes to anyone who appears to be in need.

Richard has not slept or eaten for several nights, and has been dressing in a variety of increasingly unusual outfits, which he changes several times a day. He has also been physically threatened by passers-by who have not appreciated his sudden and uninvited monologues on the works of obscure philosophers.

A homeless outreach team have managed to engage Richard and have tried, without success, to persuade him to come into hospital for a short time as they do not feel he is safe and believe that he is becoming increasingly overactive and bizarre. Richard is adamant that he will not come to hospital, and approved social workers have failed to agree that his condition warrants detention under the Mental Health Act. However, Richard has said that he would agree to come to a staffed residential placement, and he has been referred to a hostel for a short while.

✓

Richard (continued)

Richard: points for reflection

1. Is Richard 'vulnerable', and if so, why?

2. Is Richard mentally ill, or just an eccentric and exceptionally generous man?

3. How might workers at the residential placement best offer support to Richard during his stay?

Case notes: John

John is 72 years old and is a retired accountant. His wife Rose has asked their general practitioner (GP) to visit at home as her husband has refused to get out of bed for several days and, according to Rose, has been 'peculiar' for the past three or four weeks. When the GP arrives, John hides under the duvet and refuses to talk. The GP knows John well, and is puzzled by his behaviour as he is normally a sociable and humorous man in reasonably good health. When asked what Rose means by 'peculiar' she explains that her husband has become increasingly irritable and withdrawn, refusing to have anything to do with his children and grandchildren. Normally active and interested in sports and other hobbies, he had begun to watch television at all hours of the day and night, and seemed to have difficulty sleeping. His appetite had gradually disappeared and he had not eaten for several days. When asked if she had ever noticed behaviour like this before, Rose explained that he used to become very stressed at work sometimes, but 'nothing a few pints and a round of golf with his mates wouldn't cure'. She had noticed that his alcohol consumption had increased gradually over the last few months, which he said was to help him sleep.

She also informed the doctor that John's mother had suffered from depression 'on and off' for many years, but this was something of a family secret and John did not like to discuss it. He was, she described, very much 'of the old school' and did not believe that personal problems should be discussed, even with family.

Rose appeared upset and angry toward her husband, and said that she had taken to sleeping in the spare room due to her husband's irritability and tendency to get up in the early hours of the morning for a glass of brandy.

The GP returned to her practice and made an urgent referral to the local community mental health team for assessment.

John: points for reflection

1. Is John 'clinically' depressed, or is he just feeling miserable? What is the difference in this case?

2. John is a 72-year-old man. How might this affect his experience of depression, and others' ability to help him?

3. What are the potential risks involved should mental health professionals be unable to help John?

4. From the facts identified here, were there any early indications that John was becoming unwell?

Handout 1.1 Measuring mental health

Researchers, and those of us trying to interpret their data, are faced with a recurring problem that has continued to beset mental health care since the advent of 'scientific' psychiatry in the 19th century. This is a problem of definition.

According to a frequently quoted study (Goldberg and Huxley 1992) approximately one in four British adults suffer from a mental health problem at any one time. The last major national survey (Singleton *et al.* 2000) found that one in six adults suffers from a mental health problem, but uses a narrower definition of mental disorder.

Neither study records data for psychotic disorders such as schizophrenia or bipolar disorder, nor do they include personality disorder, which, according to other studies, may affect as many as one in ten of the general population (de Girolamo and Dotto 2000). Current research is demonstrating that mental health problems are perhaps far more prevalent and widespread than many of us might have imagined.

Furthermore, what trained health professionals categorize as a 'mental disorder' may not be a problem or a disorder to an individual reporting a profile of signs, symptoms and feelings. Goldberg and Huxley's 1992 study suggested that only three-quarters of their 'mentally disordered' subjects actually visited their general practitioner as a result, indicating that a small but sizeable minority of people either do not recognize a mental disorder in themselves, or if they do, do not believe that it warrants professional intervention.

So what are the systems used to categorize and define mental illness? In the United Kingdom, mental health professionals often refer to an '*ICD-10* diagnosis' to describe a patient's condition. *The International Classification of Diseases (ICD)* is the World Health Organization's (WHO) diagnostic manual, which lists all recognized (by WHO at least) diseases and disorders, including the category 'mental and behavioural disorders' (World Health Organization 1992).

The *Diagnostic and Statistical Manual of Mental Disorders* (better known as *DSM-IV*) is more often used in the United States and elsewhere in the world (American Psychiatric Association 2000). These two sets of standards are intended to provide global standards for the recognition of mental health problems for both day-to-day clinical practice and clinical researchers, although the tools used by the latter group to measure symptoms often vary from place to place and can interfere with the 'validity' of results, or in other words the ability of one set of results to be compared with those from a different research team.

ICD-10's 'Mental and Behavioural Disorders' chapter lists 99 different types of mental health problem, each of which is further sub-divided into a variety of more precise diagnoses ranging from the relatively common and well known (such as depression or schizophrenia) to more obscure diagnoses such as 'specific developmental disorders of scholastic skills'.

The idea of using classification systems and labels to describe the highly complex vagaries of the human mind often meets with fierce resistance in mental health circles. The 'medical model' of psychiatry – diagnosis, prognosis and treatment – is essentially a means of applying the same scientific principles to the study and treatment of the mind as physical medicine applies to diseases of the body. An x-ray of the mind is impossible, a blood test will reveal nothing about how a person feels, and fitting a collection of psychiatric symptoms into a precise diagnostic category does not always yield a consistent result.

In psychiatry, symptoms often overlap with one another. For example, a person with obsessive compulsive disorder may believe that if they do not switch the lights on and off a certain number of times and in a particular order then a disaster will befall them. To most, this would appear a bizarre belief to the extent that the inexperienced practitioner may label that person as 'delusional' or 'psychotic'. Similarly, a person in the early stages of Alzheimer's Disease may often experience many of the 'textbook' features of clinical depression such as low mood, poor motivation and disturbed sleep. In fact, given the tragic and predictable consequences of dementia it is unsurprising that sufferers often require treatment for depression, particularly while they retain the awareness to know that they are suffering from a degenerative condition with little or no improvement likely.

Psychiatry may often be a less than precise science, but the various diagnostic terms are commonplace in health and social care and have at least some descriptive power, although it is also important to remember that patients or clients may experience a complex array of feelings, experiences or 'symptoms' that may vary widely with the individual over time and from situation to situation.

✓

Handout 1.2 Illness or disorder?

Mental health problems can be seen as a continuum varying from normal reactions to everyday events, to serious disability requiring long-term support. The terms mental 'illness' or mental 'disorder' are often used interchangeably, but is there a difference?

Mental 'illness' is considered to have a clearly defined and recognizable onset after a period of 'normal functioning'. This is usually taken to mean a condition that begins to manifest later in life after a relatively healthy childhood, although adolescents and even children do suffer from mental illness. The meaning of 'illness' in this context might also be thought of as a condition having an organic or biological basis, which responds to medications designed to redress imbalances of chemicals such as the neurotransmitters described elsewhere. Mental health professionals usually think of mental illness as a severe and potentially debilitating condition such as schizophrenia or bipolar disorder, although someone suffering from severe depression might also be considered 'mentally ill'.

On the other hand, mental 'disorder' is a persistent but usually less debilitating condition that has at least some basis in childhood development. Typically, a disorder may be treated with medication, although psychological treatments such as counselling or group therapy are usually considered to be of at least equal importance in addressing the patient's problems. Examples of a mental disorder might include personality disorder, anxiety, obsessive compulsive disorder or less severe forms of depression.

Handout 1.3 Psychosis

The word 'psychosis' originates from the Greek words *psyche* meaning 'mind' and *osis* meaning 'condition'. It is not a diagnosis in itself but a collective term for diagnoses such as schizophrenia and bipolar disorder, and describes a collection of symptoms that usually renders the sufferer unable to maintain anything like a normal lifestyle.

A psychotic person is someone who, to a greater or lesser extent, has lost touch with the real world, often to the extent that they hold false and often troubling beliefs, or experience sounds, sights or even smells that only they can detect. For example, the person might believe that their neighbours are attempting to poison them, or that they have special powers bestowed upon them by God. They may hear voices telling them to act in certain ways, or describing them as dirty or evil. In severe circumstances the psychotic person may speak in riddles, or with jumbled words and sentences that make sense to them but not to anyone else, and may behave strangely or even, at times, dangerously. In most cases, psychosis is easily detectable to everyone except the sufferer him or herself. In other words, the sufferer has no insight into their beliefs, experiences and behaviours, which appear to them entirely normal.

Psychosis is a broad term encompassing a number of symptoms and several individual diagnoses, but is a very widely used description in mental health care and is often used to describe a set of serious mental health problems in the absence of a more specific diagnosis. Psychotic disorders include schizophrenia and bipolar disorder, although psychosis may, in some cases, be a feature of depression or dementia. Psychosis may also be a feature of physical illness, infection (toxic confusional state) or brain trauma. Psychotic episodes are occasionally associated with recreational drugs such as cannabis, ecstasy or LSD (whose hallucinogenic effects closely mimic the symptoms of psychosis itself), although this is usually short-lived and lasts only until the substance has been metabolized by the body.

The incidence (or 'morbidity') of psychotic disorders is approximately three in every 100 people, a figure that remains remarkably constant throughout the world. Some people may experience only one period of illness, while for others, psychotic episodes may reoccur at intervals throughout their adult lives.

Handout 1.4 The anti-psychiatry movement

The anti-psychiatry movement emerged in the 1960s and became a radical but popular ideology that continues to exert some influence today. The term is perhaps something of a misnomer as most of the main protagonists were medically trained psychiatrists themselves and did not advocate that mental illness did not exist or did not warrant treatment, but suggested that the traditional 'medical model' view of, for example, schizophrenia could not be accounted for by biological factors and could not be simply treated as a 'disease' like other medical disorders.

Anti-psychiatry criticized the 'social control' aspects of modern mental health care, and what was considered to be the 'inhumane' treatment of patients with treatments such as ECT and medication. Two of the most influential 'anti-psychiatry' psychiatrists were Drs R.D. Laing and Thomas Szasz.

Dr Thomas Szasz

Szasz is essentially a libertarian and proponent of freedom of choice who has written about many issues beyond mental health, although his medical background is psychiatry. He is a prolific author, best known for *The Myth of Mental Illness* (1960), in which he argues that the classification of certain behaviours as 'illness' is simply the state's way of controlling anti-social or undesirable behaviour. In Szasz's view, the 'agents' of the state are psychiatrists who, given the power to detain individuals and medicate them against their will, are responsible for containing and controlling society's less favourable individuals.

Szasz was careful to dismiss his links with anti-psychiatry and, as a practising clinician, maintained that there is nothing wrong with the treatment of mental illness where treatment is not coercive or involuntary but takes place as a partnership between patient and therapist. Szasz's call for the abolition of psychiatric hospitals and detention of the mentally ill was perhaps far too radical for widespread adoption, but has certainly inspired the emergence of mental health as a political concept and has perhaps been instrumental in the rise of mental health pressure groups and the move toward care in the community and away from some of the less desirable elements of institutional psychiatry of previous decades.

Dr R.D. Laing

As a trained psychiatrist, Ronald Laing first came to prominence in the early 1960s with his book *The Divided Self* (1960). Like Szasz, he was never comfortable with the anti-psychiatry association, but argued that the bizarre behaviour and speech of psychotic illness were manifestations of distress rather than an essentially biological phenomenon, which has been the orthodox hypothesis for several decades and continues to be the focus of schizophrenia research today as seen elsewhere in this chapter.

Laing saw hallucinations, delusions and thought disorder as a means of communication, particularly within the context of a troubled social or family environment. According to Laing, 'madness' was an appropriate and cathartic form of expression from which the individual could benefit and learn. Laing's ideas are widely dismissed today, but have led to the increasing realization that symptoms such as delusions or hallucinations often have a meaning for the individual beyond the otherwise random and bizarre, and that forms of 'talking treatments' can be highly effective for sufferers of psychosis in addition to the more usual pharmacological treatments such as anti-psychotics.

Handout 1.5 Early warning signs

Episodes of depression or psychosis rarely happen 'out of the blue' and there are often subtle, initial signs that a person is becoming psychotic. Sometimes the signs are so subtle they may go unnoticed unless the sufferer, family or carers are aware of them. These are called 'early warning signs'. People usually have more than one early warning sign and they become increasingly evident as an individual becomes more unwell. The individuals themselves may not be aware of these indicators and may deny them when discussed, but they should be reported to a GP or mental health professional when noticed.

The person's care coordinator or a mental health professional should have a clear profile of early warning signs available, as should family, carers and the general practitioner. There are a number of ways to identify early warning signs, but a profile can only be developed where there is a history of recurrent illness and the person concerned is reasonably well known to a health care professional. Some workers will utilize specific tools designed to identify early warning signs, although a simple list of relevant behaviours and/or feelings is normally sufficient, particularly for family and carers. Common early warning signs include:

- sleep problems

- changes in appearance; that is, wearing certain clothes, or becoming unusually smart or unkempt

- fixation on subjects or objects; for example, religion, politics, or a photograph

- behaviour change; for example, from sociable to quiet and withdrawn, or vice versa

- feeling threatened without due cause

- irritability.

The individual profile of such signs will vary from person to person and may include any number of behaviours or feelings that history suggests are indicative of relapse.

Early warning signs are sometimes preceded by 'trigger factors', which might include insomnia (which may be either a trigger factor or an early warning sign), key dates or anniversaries, stress, or non-compliance with medication. Awareness of trigger factors can prompt greater vigilance on the part of both the individual concerned and those around them.

Handout 1.6 Electroconvulsive therapy (ECT)

Prior to the advent of the major tranquillizers, and more sophisticated talking treatments such as cognitive behaviour therapy (CBT), the 'treatment' of mental health problems ranged from the bizarre to the positively dangerous. Most 'treatment' was of a physical nature and included cold baths, insulin-induced comas or padded cells and strait-jackets. Electroconvulsive therapy (ECT) has its origins in that era, although it is used on a strictly 'last resort' basis and is today a carefully monitored medical treatment rather than the unsophisticated and painful procedure of several decades ago.

ECT involves the passing of a small electrical current through the brain to relieve symptoms of depression and, occasionally, psychotic illness. The process is strictly controlled and administered under general anaesthetic and muscle relaxant drugs. The anaesthetized patient experiences brief seizures before being brought back to consciousness under close medical supervision. ECT is usually prescribed as a 'last resort' treatment when the patient's symptoms have not responded to more conventional treatments such as anti-depressant medication.

Despite the closely supervised nature and safeguards (National Institute for Clinical Excellence 2003), not to mention its reputation for bringing about rapid improvement in severely depressed people, ECT remains controversial and is still regarded by some as an instrument of torture rather than a bona fide medical treatment befitting the twenty-first century. The arguments surrounding the use of ECT are also fuelled by the fact that little information exists as to how it works, and side-effects of the treatment often include loss of memory (which is not normally permanent) and short-term disorientation. Most (but not all) mental health professionals regard ECT as an effective treatment where the patient is dangerously unwell or where he or she has failed to respond to more conventional treatments such as anti-depressant medication.

✓

Handout 1.7 Neurotransmitters

Serotonin

There are theories that serotonin is involved in everything from falling in love (Marazziti *et al.* 1999) to an increased risk of suicide, an association that has become increasingly controversial given the widespread prescribing of anti-depressants that increase levels of serotonin (Fergusson *et al.* 2005).

Surprisingly, most of the body's stock of serotonin is to be found in the gastro-intestinal tract rather than the brain. Although often known as a 'mood hormone' and the chemical most directly involved in the effects of ecstasy and other recreational drugs, serotonin is closely related to several forms of animal venom and performs an essential role in regulating the circulatory system.

Serotonin is closely related to sleep regulation, memory and learning as well as being largely responsible for triggering peristalsis (the passage of food through the gut). It has been known for some time that the nerve cells of depressed people have a tendency to metabolize serotonin too efficiently, leaving the brain with abnormally low levels. Modern anti-depressants (the selective serotonin reuptake inhibitors or SSRIs) block off these receptors, making more serotonin available to the brain and thus improving mood.

Noradrenaline

Noradrenaline is chemically very similar to the adrenaline most people know from the familiar 'fright, fight or flight syndrome' learnt in school biology lessons. Although noradrenaline is a vasoconstrictor (narrowing the diameter of blood vessels) and is sometimes used to treat shock and low blood pressure in emergency situations, as a nervous system neurotransmitter it has also been found to have a similar role to serotonin in regulating mood, and is associated with the psychological processes such as motivation and reward. As with serotonin, low levels of noradrenaline are associated with depression. The pathways and mechanisms of both neurotransmitters overlap with one another and several of the newer anti-depressants target both serotonin and noradrenaline receptors.

Dopamine

Dopamine is an interesting neurotransmitter closely associated with both of the above. Dopamine is one of the key agents involved in coordination and movement. The symptoms of the movement disorder Parkinson's Disease are caused by the brain's inability to produce sufficient quantities of dopamine, resulting in poor communication between the brain and the muscular system. Dopamine has an important psychological role in the experience of pleasure, and recreational drugs such as amphetamines and cocaine act on dopamine receptors, making more dopamine available to the brain. It is also closely associated with cognitive processes such as memory, attention and problem-solving, and is believed to play an important role in the mind's association between stimuli and reward. Recent theories suggest that dopamine influences our tendency to look forward to experiences we know to be pleasurable, as well as highlighting potentially threatening or dangerous things.

Dopamine overactivity is well known to be associated with the symptoms of psychosis. Anti-psychotic drugs work by blocking dopamine receptors. However, older types of anti-psychotics tended to be somewhat over-zealous in this respect, sometimes resulting in side-effects that resembled the tremor and other symptoms of Parkinson's Disease. Newer 'atypical' anti-psychotics are more selective in their blocking action, less sedating and target a wider range of symptoms than their predecessors.

✓

Mental health

- Mental health problems affect between a quarter and a sixth of the population depending on definition of mental health problem.

- Only a small minority of those receiving treatment are admitted as in-patients.

- Mental disorder: a persistent but usually less debilitating condition that has at least some basis in childhood development.

- Mental illness: a clearly defined and recognizable onset after a period of normal functioning.

Schizophrenia

- not a 'split' personality but a 'destruction' of the personality
- difficulties with normal lifestyle; for example, relationships, career, housing etc.
- incidence of 1 per cent worldwide
- emergence usually during late adolescence/early adulthood
- pre-morbid personality usually shy, withdrawn, socially awkward.

Signs and symptoms

- loss of insight; for example, 'I'm not ill!'
- delusions: beliefs not supported by culture or circumstances; for example, 'Hidden microphones are recording me!'
- thought disorder: jumbled thoughts and speech, difficulty in following normal line of conversation
- hallucinations: a false sensory perception in the absence of an external stimulus; for example, 'hearing voices'
- negative symptoms: apathy, social withdrawal.

Schizophrenia: causes (aetiology)

The brain

- excess dopamine, abnormal levels of serotonin

- abnormal brain structures; for example, enlarged ventricles.

Heredity

- strong genetic links but not a causative factor in its own right

- high risk of future illness for child with two schizophrenic parents.

The environment

- anti-psychiatry movement precedes expressed emotion theory

- low expressed emotion (LEE) = carers relaxed, non-judgemental attitudes

- high expressed emotion (HEE) = carers confrontational, judgemental

- LEE = improved outcomes for schizophrenia

- HEE = worsening of symptoms, higher risk of relapse.

Bipolar disorder

- a psychotic disorder perhaps better known as manic depression
- periods of functional and emotional stability interspersed with episodes of mania and depression
- rapid cycling form more debilitating and disruptive
- usual onset late adolescence/early twenties.

Mania

- a period of elation, overactivity, and grandiose beliefs
- often triggered by stress or adverse life events
- disorganization, overspending, rapid incomprehensible speech
- usually requires in-patient treatment if severe.

Depression

- polar opposite of mania (hence 'bipolar')
- more rapid onset than 'unipolar' depression
- tendency for more severe symptoms than unipolar depression
- high suicide risk
- often requires in-patient admission.

Causes of bipolar disorder

- no single cause: combination of 'nurture' and 'nature' explanations?
- high incidence of emotional trauma in childhood
- possible similarities to expressed emotion theory of schizophrenia
- abnormal brain structures revealed by scanning techniques such as positron emission tomography (PET)
- strong genetic link.

✓

Depression (unipolar)

- feelings of prolonged, severe despair that impair normal functioning and quality of life

- varies widely in intensity from mild symptoms to 'catatonia'

- cannot simply 'snap out of it'

- low mood, low self-esteem, apathy, lack of energy, loss of appetite, sleep disturbances, poor concentration.

Causes

- no single cause identified

- symptoms associated with lack of neurotransmitter serotonin

- also associated with stress, life events and childhood trauma.

Chapter 2
Treatment and Support

While today's mental health environment is as much about support and care as 'treatment' in the strictly medical sense, the treatments and therapies on offer remain widely misunderstood and, in some cases, controversial. This chapter outlines some of the most widely used methods in the treatment of mental illness.

Medication

Psychiatric drugs are somewhat unfairly castigated by some, and have attracted negative publicity and equally negative imagery for many years. Nonetheless, with careful prescribing and administration, anti-psychotics, tranquillizers, anti-depressants and others do have a valuable role to play in mental health care alongside the support of family, friends and professionals, and some of the 'talking treatments' we shall be looking at later in this section.

Most of the drugs used specifically in mental health care can be classified as belonging to one of several main groups. As if the huge variety of drugs, dosages and preparations were not confusing enough, medicines are usually known by 1. 'brand' names and 2. 'generic' or 'proprietary' names. For example, 'Prozac' is now one of the best-known drugs in the world, but very few people would recognize the same preparation by its generic title 'fluoxetine'.

Pharmacists, prescribers and mental health professionals are generally encouraged to use the generic names of drugs, as one preparation may have more than one brand name, particularly if it has been on the market for more than a few years.

Typical anti-psychotics

Rather misleadingly, the 'typical' anti-psychotics are often referred to as 'major tranquillizers'. This group of drugs is designed to target the areas of the brain responsible for psychotic phenomena such as thought disorder, hallucinations and so on. Chlorpromazine, the first anti-psychotic drug, was first used in the 1950s and preceded a number of other anti-psychotic drugs that worked by blocking some of the brain's dopamine receptors (see Chapter 1, Handout 1.7 Neurotransmitters), thus reducing the concentration of this chemical and clearing some of the more distressing symptoms of illnesses such as schizophrenia. Although chlorpromazine, haloperidol and their ilk have been widely and effectively used for many years, one serious drawback of the typical anti-psychotics is their tendency to cause serious side-effects (National Collaborating Centre for Mental Health 2002), some of which resemble the symptoms of Parkinson's Disease, which is itself associated with a lack of dopamine.

Typical anti-psychotics also have quite powerful sedative effects, and are sometimes used for this purpose for people whose symptoms lead to restlessness, agitation or aggression, hence the term 'major tranquillizers'. In less acute circumstances, however, the sedation caused by chlorpromazine or haloperidol combined with the low mood, apathy and social withdrawal often associated with mental illness is obviously less than desirable, and is a major cause of non-compliance with drug treatment.

Although still in use, the prescription of typical anti-psychotics is becoming less widespread and is being increasingly replaced by the more sophisticated 'atypical' preparations. Examples of typical anti-psychotics include:

- chlorpromazine (Largactil)

- thioridazine (Melleril)[*]

- trifluoperazine (Stelazine)

- haloperidol (Haldol or Serenace)

- droperidol (Droleptan).

DEPOT INJECTIONS

Depot injections are long-term versions of the tablet or syrup medications, and are normally given by injection into the upper part of the buttock. The active ingredient of depot injections is released slowly from the fatty deposits around the injection site over a period of between two to four weeks, although the injection interval may occasionally be more frequent.

Examples of depot injections include:

- zuclopenthixol decanoate (Clopixol)

- fluphenazine decanoate (Modecate)

- flupenthixol decanoate (Depixol).

Atypical anti-psychotics

These drugs operate in much the same way as the 'typical' anti-psychotics, but are much more precise in the way they reduce excess dopamine. In fact, the atypicals can be thought of as a generally more sophisticated treatment of

---

[*]   No longer licensed for general use in the UK.

psychotic symptoms, and use much of the more recent research into the role of brain chemicals and pathways to counter symptoms of conditions such as schizophrenia and bipolar disorder.

Some of the atypicals also help counter the so-called 'negative' symptoms of schizophrenia such as social withdrawal and apathy by altering levels of neurotransmitters such as serotonin. Subsequently, they are less likely to produce unpleasant side-effects and are less sedating than their more traditional counterparts. Examples of atypical anti-psychotic drugs include:

- olanzapine (Zyprexa)

- risperidone (Risperdal)

- quetiapine (Seroquel)

- aripiprazole (Abilify)

- clozapine (Clozaril).

Clozapine is an atypical anti-psychotic, which was first used to treat schizophrenia only several years after the discovery of chlorpromazine. However, while it is highly effective in treating severe mental illness, it can cause side-effects such as weight gain, seizures or a blood disorder called neutropenia, which reduces a person's ability to fight infection. For this reason its use is reserved for people who have not responded to, or are intolerant of, other treatments and requires regular blood testing and very careful management by doctors and mental health professionals.

Anxiolytics

The term 'anxiolytic' is usually used to refer to any drug treatment aimed at reducing anxiety. Of course, as anyone who has tried public speaking will testify, anxiety is a very normal and usually short-lived reaction to stressful events. But for some people, anxiety is a chronic, debilitating problem that prevents the sufferer from performing even everyday tasks. Anxiolytics are often confused with 'tranquillizers', although some of the drugs listed here could not be described as tranquillizers in the normal sense.

BENZODIAZEPINES

Drugs such as diazepam (e.g. Valium) or lorazepam (e.g. Ativan) are among the best known anxiolytics and belong to a class of drugs known as benzodiazepines. Often referred to as 'benzos' by drug addicts, and 'minor tranquillizers' by mental health professionals, drugs such as diazepam are quite sought-after as drugs of abuse and their rapid effect and potential for creating dependence make the benzodiazepines anything but 'minor'. Although no longer licensed in the UK, flunitrazepam has gained recent notoriety under the better-known guise of Rohypnol, the so-called 'date rape' drug.

Patients develop 'tolerance' to benzodiazepines quite quickly, requiring larger doses over time in order to gain the same calming effect. Nonetheless, prescribed responsibly and over a short period of time the benzodiazepines offer useful quick-acting sedation for people in severe distress and anxiety, allowing the potential for the person to discuss their feelings and talk through the problems that have caused the distress before their situation becomes uncontrollable. Drugs such as chlordiazepoxide (Librium) have long provided a mainstay of treatment for those undergoing detoxification from alcohol. Examples of commonly used benzodiazepine anxiolytics include:

- chlordiazepoxide (Librium)

- diazepam (Valium and others)

- lorazepam (Ativan)

- oxazepam (Serenid).

OTHER ANXIOLYTICS

Beta-blockers such as propanolol (Inderal) and oxprenolol (Trasicor) are better known as 'blood pressure tablets' than anxiolytics, and are usually prescribed to people with hypertension or cardiac problems. However, they are sometimes useful in the treatment of anxiety, particularly as they are in many ways less harmful than the benzodiazepines. They work by 'damping down' the physical effects of adrenaline and noradrenaline (the 'fight, flight and fright' hormones) and therefore reducing the psychological effects of anxiety.

We should also mention another anxiolytic called buspirone (Buspar), which belongs to a class of drug known as the 'azaspirodecanediones'. We needn't worry too much about the latter or try to pronounce it; suffice to say that buspirone depresses anxiety on a long-term basis in a way not dissimilar to the SSRI anti-depressants (see below) and is not normally dependence-inducing like the benzodiazepines.

Anti-depressants

As the name suggests, an anti-depressant is a drug used in combating the most debilitating effects of clinical depression. Contrary to some beliefs, anti-depressants are not 'happy pills' and have no 'street' or recreational value. They are of little use in cases of short-term grief or as 'pick me ups' for adverse events as they take several weeks to have any demonstrable effect, but can be invaluable in situations where the symptoms of depression described earlier in this chapter have prevented an individual from leading a normal life.

There is now a bewildering array of anti-depressants on the market, and brands such as Prozac have become as well known as Aspirin or Valium, which is often mistakenly referred to as an anti-depressant. There are, broadly speaking, two main classes of anti-depressant commonly prescribed by GPs and psychiatrists.

TRICYCLIC ANTI-DEPRESSANTS

Tricyclic anti-depressants have been available for many years, and work on making more of the neurotransmitters serotonin and noradrenaline available, both of which are important in regulating mood. However, tricyclics take a rather indiscriminate approach to chemical regulation and can cause quite pronounced drowsiness and symptoms of dehydration such as blurred vision and dry mouth. Some tricyclics are also known to be dangerous in overdose, and many prescribers now prefer to use the SSRI-type drugs (see below) to treat depression. Examples of tricyclic anti-depressants include:

- amitriptyline (Tryptizol)

- clomipramine (Anafranil)

- dothiepin (Prothiaden)

- imipramine (Tofranil)

- lofepramine (Gamanil)

- trimipramine (Surmontil).

SELECTIVE SEROTONIN REUPTAKE INHIBITORS (SSRIs)

While working in much the same way as the tricyclics, the SSRIs are more (as the name suggests) selective in the way they work and some SSRIs also affect neurotransmitters such as noradrenaline and other brain pathways. These drugs are generally less toxic in overdose, and patients report fewer and less severe side-effects. Like the tricyclics, benefits depend on a certain therapeutic level of the drug building up in the patient's bloodstream and positive effects will not usually be seen for several weeks following the first dose. The widespread and sometimes inappropriate prescribing of some SSRIs has attracted criticism in the United Kingdom, particularly with regard to the number of children and adolescents now prescribed SSRI drugs, a practice that is now tightly regulated (Medicines and Healthcare Products Regulatory Agency 2004).

Paroxetine (Seroxat) has gained a certain notoriety for allegedly causing dependence and behaviour change in patients. It is sometimes difficult to distinguish the perceived negative effects of a psychoactive drug from the symptoms of mental disorder itself, a fact that has complicated the research into the potentially harmful effects of drugs such as paroxetine and fluoxetine. While prescribing safeguards are now beginning to appear in legislation, it should also be remembered that SSRIs are taken effectively and without problem by many thousands of people throughout the world (National Collaborating Centre for Mental Health 2004). Examples of SSRIs include:

- citalopram (Cipramil)

- fluoxetine (Prozac)

- paroxetine (Seroxat)

- sertraline (Lustral)

- mirtazapine (Zispin).

Mood stabilizers

People with bipolar disorder are usually treated with drugs that help stabilize the extremes of mood (mania and depression) that characterize this illness. They are not a 'cure' for bipolar disorder but are helpful in maintaining stability, or what mental health professionals call a 'baseline mental state'. Studies have shown that extremes of mood and relapse are much more common when sufferers remain untreated, although as we have already seen, diagnosis is often difficult and compliance with medication is sometimes compromised by the symptoms of the illness itself and the unsurprising reluctance of many bipolar sufferers to submit themselves to life-long medication (Jones, Hayward and Lam 2002).

Mood stabilizers do not belong to any particular chemical type. Two of the most commonly used treatments are better known as anti-epileptic drugs, and perhaps the best known, lithium (Priadel, Camcolit or unbranded), is actually a metal. The atypical anti-psychotic olanzapine (Zyprexa) has recently been licensed in the UK as a mood stabilizer. The dissimilarity of the drugs used to treat bipolar disorder reflect the vagaries of the illness itself, and prescribers need to carefully control or 'titrate' doses and medications in accordance with the nature of the patient's illness. Furthermore, combinations of different mood stabilizers may sometimes need to be prescribed where one medication, or 'monotherapy', is not maintaining stability alone.

Lithium in particular needs careful monitoring. In high concentrations it can be toxic and its levels are measured by regular blood tests. Patients are advised not to become dehydrated (a particular risk for heavy drinkers) and to take medical advice before taking other prescribed or 'over the counter' medicines. Any signs of physical ill-health in patients taking lithium should be reported to health professionals immediately. Examples of mood stabilizers include:

- sodium valproate (Epilim)

- carbamazepine (Tegretol)

- lithium carbonate (Priadel)

- olanzapine (Zyprexa).

Talking treatments

Otherwise known variously as counselling, psychotherapy, or just plain 'therapy', the talking treatments enable patients to resolve problems by working through issues on a one-to-one or group basis, usually led by a professional person. While there are many and varied types of talking treatments in use, some of the more widely used and well-established therapies are outlined here.

Cognitive behaviour therapy (CBT)

The basis of CBT is that an individual's thoughts, feelings and behaviour are closely linked, and that if we can change the way a person thinks then we can also alter and improve the way they feel and what they do. CBT has been found to be as effective a treatment for mild to moderate depression as anti-depressant drugs, and normally requires little more than a few months or even weeks of hourly sessions, sometimes with occasional 'top up' and review sessions (National Collaborating Centre for Mental Health 2004).

Depressed or anxious individuals tend to think in negatives, and believe that the glass is always half empty or that toast always lands butter side down. For example, a successful business person may have a 'mindset' of self-confidence, risk-taking and a 'can do' philosophy. On the other hand, a career criminal's mind may be 'programmed' to think negatively, to have little self-belief or that everything bad is either their fault, or alternately the fault of everyone except themselves.

These core beliefs dramatically affect an individual's day-to-day life, but a cognitive behaviour therapist makes detailed records of a person's thoughts, beliefs and actions and helps the patient challenge their own negative thoughts and beliefs, and attempts to turn these around so that the person develops a more positive outlook and becomes more optimistic.

Cognitive behaviour therapy is quite different from many other types of therapy in that it is short term, highly focussed and deals more with the 'here and now' rather than concentrating on links with the past or attempting to explain 'why' the patient feels a certain way.

Counselling/psychotherapy

There are dozens of different forms and theories of counselling and psychotherapy. The easiest description of counselling is that it is a process of spending time with another person and perhaps helping them find their own solutions to one or more difficult issues. Therefore, most people probably engage in some form of counselling on an informal, day-to-day basis, whether with clients, friends or members of the family.

Most carers and mental health professionals use basic counselling skills in their work with clients, although very few have a specific qualification. Professional counsellors and psychotherapists have studied for several years, and have often undergone therapy themselves as part of their training. In practice, there is a great deal of overlap between professional counselling and psychotherapy, although most practitioners would suggest that counselling focuses on specific issues (such as bereavement or addiction) while psychotherapy is a more 'in-depth' process of self-discovery.

People in distress can often get significant benefit from talking to a trusted individual who has the ability to 'actively listen' to what they have to say. This is, in effect, counselling. It doesn't necessarily require 'knowing what to say' or making insightful interpretations of a person's behaviour, as it is the counsellor's role to help the person find their own solutions, not give advice.

Group therapy

Group therapy is not a specific treatment approach like CBT, but is better described as an umbrella term for a number of different therapy styles conducted with a group of clients rather than an individual. Any of the treatment approaches described previously can be conducted within a group setting, and many people attend regular group sessions dealing with, for example, substance dependence, bereavement or coping with long-term illness. In purely practical terms, group therapy is cheaper and more 'time-efficient' than individual treatment. It is therefore widely used in public sector organizations, but while some people will prefer to deal with their problems in a one-to-one situation, others will describe how valuable sharing problems with others in a group can be, and how reassuring it is to find others who have experienced similar problems or feelings.

While many groups will be led by a qualified therapist and focus on particular treatment goals, the 'group therapy' concept has now mushroomed into wider society in the form of self-help groups. One of the oldest and best known of these is Alcoholics Anonymous, whose meetings are not 'facilitated' by a therapist but led by the members, who are themselves attempting to recover from an addiction to alcohol.

The professionals: health, social and the non-statutory services

Mental health care in the UK is carried out by a wide variety of organizations, some of whom are 'statutory' (i.e. provided and managed by the National Health

Service or local authority) and some of whom are 'non-statutory' or 'voluntary'. Examples of the latter group might be charities or housing associations that provide services for mentally ill people independently of 'the state', although they will usually complement and work closely with the statutory services and will have to work within a legal framework such as the Registered Care Homes Act.

The community mental health team (CMHT)

In this section we are going to focus on those statutory services that are responsible for most 'front-line' mental health care in the community: the community mental health team or CMHT. All the professions outlined here will also feature in hospital-based mental health care, although most individual practitioners tend to be based in either in-patient or community settings, and form part of what is known as a 'secondary care' service (see Handout 2.1 The National Health Service and mental health: primary, secondary or tertiary?).

The CMHT is a multi-disciplinary team usually comprising a core group of professionals such as psychiatrists, nurses, social workers, clinical psychologists and occupational therapists. Not all teams work in the same way and other workers often form part of the team to provide practical support and assistance to both patients and qualified staff, or may lead specific projects such as job clubs, cafes, horticultural nurseries or painting and decorating groups.

Each CMHT will cover a locality that is designated as a defined area on a map, or as a collection of GP surgeries. The way in which local CMHTs work will vary widely from team to team and area to area depending on the nature of the catchment area. For example, a rural CMHT will usually cover a wide geographical area and may work in a very different way from a team based in a densely populated urban area. Local demographic factors such as affluence, age and ethnicity will also influence working practices, so it is very difficult to describe the 'typical' CMHT as they are far from homogeneous! One feature virtually all team members share is their responsibility to act as a 'care coordinator' under the auspices of the care programme approach (see Handout 2.2 The care programme approach). While CMHT patients may be involved with several different professions at any one time, their care coordinator acts as the main point of contact for that person and will be responsible for preparing and facilitating a plan of care for each patient on their caseload.

There are many myths and misunderstandings surrounding the roles of the various mental health professionals, and this section outlines the roles and responsibilities of the various disciplines. It should be pointed out that some teams work with professionals whose boundaries are very clear, while others take a more 'generic' approach where all team members undertake a variety of tasks within the team more or less irrespective of their professional background.

THE PSYCHIATRIST

A psychiatrist is a medically qualified doctor who has undertaken several years' further training in psychiatry. To specialize in this field a psychiatrist will have qualified for membership of the Royal College of Psychiatrists. Most (but not all) CMHTs are led by a consultant psychiatrist and he or she will have responsibility for diagnosis, pharmocological treatment and overall management of patient care. Like other mental health professionals a psychiatrist might practise as a general clinician while others may undertake further specialist training in areas such as eating disorders, forensic psychiatry (the assessment and treatment of mentally disordered offenders) or child and adolescent mental health.

Unlike other members of the team, psychiatrists will usually work in both in-patient and community settings, and may often have an allocated number of beds at a psychiatric unit to which they can admit patients.

Most of the powers to detain individuals under the Mental Health Act require a doctor's assessment, although those parts of the Act that determine compulsory treatment must be sanctioned by a psychiatrist specially approved under Section 12 of the Mental Health Act (see Appendix: Introducing the Mental Health Act 1983). If the patient is subject to the Mental Health Act, the 'responsible medical officer' has a legal as well as clinical responsibility including decisions around the detention, discharge and leave accorded to the patient.

Psychiatrists are often portrayed in the media as 'talking therapists' who see their patients on couches and make interpretations of their behaviour based on childhood events. In reality, while some psychiatrists are trained in various 'talking treatments', most perform much the same role as doctors in other medical specialisms in that they diagnose mental health problems and prescribe an appropriate course of treatment if necessary.

THE CLINICAL PSYCHOLOGIST

Trained psychologists exist in many guises. Some remain within the academic world after graduating and conduct research studies on how the human mind thinks, feels, reacts and makes decisions, or how individuals perform within groups or how groups interact with other groups. Much of our current understanding of mental disorder comes from the field of neuropsychology, where responses and actions are compared with detailed 'real time' brain scanning. Psychologists also work in business, industry, advertising and sport, but a 'clinical' psychologist treats patients and works directly with mental health problems using a variety of specialized techniques. They are skilled in the use of a range of diagnostic tests and tools, and may carry out a wide range of treatments, particularly the 'talking treatments' we have looked at earlier. Clinical psychologists also provide training and supervision in this kind of work to other professionals.

Clinical psychologists are often confused with psychiatrists, especially by the media. Sometimes a clinical psychologist will have a post-graduate research degree such as a PhD and will therefore have the prefix 'Dr', but is not qualified in medicine. Clinical psychologists must have a degree in psychology plus a further qualification in clinical work.

THE COMMUNITY PSYCHIATRIC NURSE (CPN)

Community psychiatric nurses (CPNs) are qualified mental health nurses, some of whom have completed specialist training for community work. Most CMHTs include several CPNs and form the most numerous workforce of all the disciplines. They work in an increasingly wide range of situations with a diverse patient group. While some work with patients referred by a local GP, others work within substance dependence clinics, with the street homeless, or in prisons. They are responsible for helping patients with practical problems, and are often qualified in delivering different types of therapy such as behaviour therapy or counselling. They are sometimes responsible for both the administration and management of medicines (particularly the depot anti-psychotics outlined earlier) and helping patients understand both their diagnosis and the treatment they are receiving.

THE MENTAL HEALTH SOCIAL WORKER (MHSW)

Social workers are another professional group whose role is often misunderstood. The mental health social worker (MHSW) is a key member of the CMHT although, unlike many of their colleagues, he or she is usually employed by the local authority rather than the local NHS trust.

MHSWs have a general qualification in social work and have specialized later in mental health. They coordinate and monitor care plans, and are often responsible for managing and budgeting for a complete package of care including services such as housing, work retraining or benefits advice. Their training and work experience often leads to work with families, where one family member's mental health problems may be leading to problems within the family as a whole, or where the family are acting as 'carers' and require support to carry out this role.

Approved social workers (ASWs) are specially trained MHSWs with responsibility for assessing individuals who may warrant detention under the Mental Health Act, and preparing reports for tribunals.

THE OCCUPATIONAL THERAPIST

Occupational therapists undergo three years' training prior to qualification and work in a range of settings beyond mental health. Their role within the multi-disciplinary team is to assess patients' skills and functioning using specific tools, and based on that assessment develop occupational treatment programmes. The programmes are regularly reviewed to measure changes in the patients' functioning and are adapted accordingly.

For some people with an enduring mental illness such as depression or schizophrenia, isolation and loss of motivation are key issues along with impaired ability to carry out everyday tasks such as cooking, shopping, going to work or looking after a house. Occupational therapy helps patients to improve skills they may have lost due to illness, and to develop coping strategies for returning to a more normal way of life.

The non-statutory services

Large psychiatric hospitals (or 'asylums') have been in the process of closing down since the early 1960s, with the 1990 Community Care Act accelerating the process to the point that today's mental health care is largely delivered in the patient's own locality. Many of the services once provided solely by health and social services professionals are now delivered by a wide variety of organizations. In particular, a number of charities and special needs housing associations offer support, advice and practical help in addition to meeting basic needs such as housing. These agencies are now working closely with the statutory sector (health and social services) and in many cases receive the bulk of their funding from government and local authorities. Examples of services provided by non-statutory agencies include housing, day care, employment schemes, advice centres and telephone helplines.

References

Jones, S., Hayward, P. and Lam, D. (2002) *Coping with Bipolar Disorder: A Guide to Living with Manic Depression.* Oxford: Oneworld Publications.

Medicines and Healthcare products Regulatory Agency (MHRA) (2004) *Selective Serotonin Reuptake Inhibitors (SSRIs): Overview of Regulatory Status and CSM Advice Relating to Major Depressive Disorder (MDD) in Children and Adolescents Including a Summary of Available Safety and Efficacy Data.* London: MHRA.

National Collaborating Centre for Mental Health (2002) *Schizophrenia: Core Interventions in the Treatment and Management of Schizophrenia in Primary and Secondary Care.* London: National Institute for Clinical Excellence.

National Collaborating Centre for Mental Health (2004) *Depression: Management of Depression in Primary and Secondary Care.* London: National Institute for Clinical Excellence.

Useful resources

Websites

Medication Guide: Norfolk and Waveney Mental Health Partnership NHS Trust: www.nmhct.nhs.uk/pharmacy

Mental Health Care: www.mentalhealthcare.org.uk

National Institute for Clinical Excellence: www.nice.org.uk

National Institute for Mental Health in England: www.nimhe.org.uk/home

Royal College of Psychiatrists: www.rcpsych.ac.uk

Books

Healy, D. (2004a) *Psychiatric Drugs Explained*. Edinburgh: Churchill Livingstone.

Healy, D. (2004b) *The Creation of Psychopharmacology*. Cambridge, MA: Harvard University Press.

Parrott, A. (2004) *Understanding Drugs and Behaviour*. Chichester: John Wiley and Sons.

Handout 2.1 The National Health Service and mental health: primary, secondary or tertiary?

The NHS can be seen as a three-tier process comprised of three distinct layers: primary, secondary and tertiary care.

Primary health care

The primary health care system is the network of general practice surgeries serving local communities. A practice usually includes at least one general practitioner (GP) together with a variety of other health care professionals (such as practice nurses, physiotherapists, chiropodists, etc.) providing treatments and other medical services. Some (but by no means all) practices employ community psychiatric nurses (CPNs) and qualified counsellors.

Primary health currently provides a substantial proportion of mental health care for those with less severe disorders. Counsellors and CPNs will see patients referred by their GPs who may be suffering anxiety or depression of a type that does not necessarily warrant intervention from a community mental health team (CMHT), and GPs will often prescribe anxiolytics or anti-depressants while monitoring a patient's symptoms over a period of time, only referring to more specialist assessment in cases where the situation worsens or problems remain intractable for substantial periods of time.

Secondary health care

Secondary health care is the terminology applied to specialist treatments usually provided by a hospital or clinic. A GP refers to a specialist in secondary health care for more detailed assessment or specialist treatment such as surgery. CMHTs form part of the secondary health care system, as do in-patient psychiatric units and hospitals.

Tertiary health care

'Tertiary' refers to the most specialized level of care, examples of which include services such as eating disorder teams, or forensic psychiatric services that work with mentally disordered offenders.

Handout 2.2 The care programme approach

The care programme approach (CPA) was introduced in 1991 by an Act of Parliament the previous year (Community Care Act 1990) and is intended to be the basis for the care of people with mental health needs outside hospital. It applies to all people with mental health problems who are accepted as clients of specialist mental health services.

In many cases, the CPA comes into play while someone is a psychiatric hospital in-patient (not necessarily detained under the Mental Health Act), and creates the framework for discharge planning and after-care. The CPA also links in with care management practised by local authority social services departments, where social services departments are undertaking their duties of assessing needs and purchasing appropriate services, under the NHS and Community Care Act. CPA, care management and (where applicable) Section 117 duties (see Appendix: Introducing the Mental Health Act 1983) can be integrated into a single process.

The CPA process has four stages:

- a systematic assessment of the person's health care and social care needs

- the development of a care plan agreed by all involved, including the person her/himself and any informal carers, as far as this is possible, and addressing the assessed needs

- identifying a care coordinator to be the main point of contact with the person concerned and to monitor the delivery of the care plan

- regular review of the person's progress and the care plan, with agreed changes to the plan as required.

✓

Medication

- Medications used to treat mental illness belong to one of six main groups. These are:
    - typical anti-psychotics; for example, chlorpromazine
    - atypical anti-psychotics; for example, olanzapine
    - anxiolytics; for example, diazepam
    - tricyclic anti-depressants; for example, amitriptyline
    - selective serotonin reuptake inhibitors (SSRIs); for example, fluoxetine
    - mood stabilizers; for example, lithium carbonate.

- Medications are known by two names:
    1. 'generic' or 'proprietary' name; for example, diazepam
    2. 'brand' name; for example, Valium.

Talking treatments

Cognitive behaviour therapy (CBT)

- thoughts, feelings and behaviour are linked, and with practice can be modified and improved

- a highly effective treatment for mild to moderate depression

- challenges 'negative' thoughts

- short term, highly focussed and deals with the 'here and now'.

Counselling/psychotherapy

- many different forms and theories

- a process of spending time with another person and helping them find their own solutions and deal with difficult issues

- involves 'active listening'

- counselling focuses on specific issues

- psychotherapy: 'an in-depth process of self-discovery'.

Group therapy

- an 'umbrella term' for a number of different therapy styles

- takes place in a group with group leaders and members contributing to the therapeutic process.

✓

The professionals: community mental health teams

- multi-disciplinary team comprising a core group of professionals; for example, psychiatrists, nurses, occupational therapists, social workers and clinical psychologists

- covers 'localities'

- a 'statutory' service; that is, governmental.

The psychiatrist

- medically qualified doctor training to be, or existing member of, the Royal College of Psychiatrists

- responsible for diagnosis and pharmacological treatment

- consultant psychiatrist: responsible for overall management of patient care

- works in both in-patient and community settings.

The clinical psychologist

- skilled in the use of a wide range of diagnostic tests and tools

- facilitates and supervises psychological therapies; for example, cognitive behaviour therapy

- may have a post-graduate research degree and so have the prefix 'Dr' but is not medically trained

- possesses a degree in psychology plus a further qualification in clinical work.

The community psychiatric nurse (CPN)

- qualified psychiatric nurse
- works in a wide range of situations with a diverse patient group
- often qualified in delivering different types of therapy
- may administer depot anti-psychotic medications and helps patients manage medication
- helps patients understand their illness.

The mental health social worker (MHSW)

- usually employed by a local authority rather than NHS trust
- possesses a general qualification in social work before specializing in mental health
- further training required to become an approved social worker (ASW)
- ASW responsible for assessing patients who may require detention under the Mental Health Act, and providing reports for tribunal hearings.

The occupational therapist

- works in a range of settings
- assesses skills and functioning using specific tools and designs occupational treatment programmes
- helps clients to improve work and life skills and to develop coping strategies for returning to a more normal way of life
- works with both individuals and groups.

✓

The professionals: non-statutory services

- replace many services once provided solely by health and social services professionals

- include charities, housing associations and special needs care providers

- offer support, advice and practical help in addition to meeting basic needs such as housing

- work closely with the statutory sector (health and social services) and in many cases receive funding from government and local authorities.

Chapter 3
Risk Assessment and Management

In its broadest sense, the term 'risk' represents the delicate balance between the potential benefit of a proposed action and the potential harm that action may cause. In mental health terms, this means providing clients with as much choice, freedom and opportunity as possible while being aware that people with mental health problems do sometimes harm themselves or other people. Mental health carers are charged daily with the responsibility of using the evidence available to us to balance opportunities against threat, and to work with clients on a plan of care that reflects this balance.

While even the most diligent care, support and supervision will not prevent the occasional but inevitable untoward event, a growing library of inquiry reports into tragedies such as homicides or suicides suggest that events such as these often arise from failures of health care, social services, housing and voluntary sector agencies to 'prevent the preventable' (Sheppard 1996). The challenge for both organizations and individual professionals is the achievement of a balance between safe management on the one hand, and improving quality of life on the other.

With the application of some basic skills in the assessment and management of risk, workers can at least make an informed decision as to the likelihood and potential severity of untoward events, and care plans can be developed that allow such events to happen as seldom as possible within the resources available.

Many individuals will present no form of risk at all, and the thorough processes described here may appear superfluous. But for people who are known to have been aggressive, suicidal or have put themselves at risk through a worsening of their mental state or erratic lifestyle, risk assessment and management is an undoubtedly essential aspect of our overall care.

This part of the book is an attempt to outline some of the most important principles in risk assessment and management. As yet there appears to be no 'industry standard' model in widespread use, and every organization will have developed its own policies and procedures in assessing and managing risk, so the guidance offered here is broad-ranging and intended to suggest good practice rather than propose any specific framework.

What is risk assessment?

The assessment of risk involves the identification of factors and circumstances that may contribute to an untoward incident or situation. The aim is to avoid harm to both the client or other persons, which may come in the form of self-harm, suicide, violence toward others, self-neglect or exploitation.

The risk involved in a car driver's insurance premiums may be calculated on the basis of precise mathematical formulae, but mental health risk assessment is not a statistical process. It is impossible to accurately predict the probability that Client A will perform Action X within a given period of time. But through a process of careful risk assessment, it *is* possible to identify factors that, in collaboration with the client, our colleagues and other agencies, can be managed so as to minimize the possibility of harm.

It is, however, important to remember that tragic and unfortunate events can, and do, happen. Risk assessment demands the answer to certain key questions. This chapter outlines these questions along with the reasons for asking them, but we are likely to be asking difficult, searching questions of both the client themselves and others who have known him or her. Despite the plethora of tools, models, forms and policies that have appeared in recent years, risk assessment is far from the simple 'paper exercise' it may first appear, and is above all an opportunity to develop and use communication and rapport-building skills as well as one's own experience and intuition.

Finally, risk assessment is sometimes perceived as an 'event' or 'task' that is carried out at a fixed time, often at the start of an agency's contact with a new client. While initial contact will certainly involve some form of referral, information gathering and usually a meeting with the subject of the referral (see Handout 3.1 First contact), risk assessment can be more accurately described as an ongoing and dynamic *process* incorporating factors that change constantly with time and circumstance, and will constantly guide the assessment and management of the potential risks posed.

Identifying risk factors

The identification of risk factors can be thought of initially as a process of information gathering or collation, in particular the key areas of history and background that will best inform our awareness of an individual and the potential risks involved.

Resources may be limited, and some prioritization may be a useful means of determining the resources devoted to the risk assessment process, although how the combination of degree and likelihood is managed will be determined by each organization's own policies and procedures.

Without doubt, the key to any good risk assessment process is history and information. A truly thorough risk assessment will demand time, resources and persistence, particularly where clients have arrived with a poorly documented or chaotic history.

The following factors are not exhaustive, but will usually form the key elements of a comprehensive assessment process.

Mental health

It is often assumed (especially by those sceptical of care in the community) that violence and suicide are inextricably linked with mental illness, and while statistics tell us this is a considerable misinterpretation (Taylor and Gunn 1999), some of the individuals we work with will have a history of mental health problems that are associated with aggression, self-injury or severe neglect. Where the client has had recent contact with health or social services, a care programme approach care plan (see Chapter 2, Handout 2.2 The care programme approach) should be available containing most of the required details. If the client is not known to us, then the first point of contact other than the client him or herself will be the care coordinator or at least someone who has the most up-to-date knowledge of that individual's care.

A history of mental health problems will include at the very least a diagnosis or some description of the individual's experience of mental illness, and how that history has interacted with any risk behaviours. For example, an individual with a history of depression may have attempted suicide in the past, or may have experienced episodes of mania during which they have made themselves vulnerable to sexual exploitation.

The client will obviously be able to provide the most intuitive information, but at times a precise chronological history may be unavailable from the individual due to cognitive impairment, their mental state, or difficulties understanding and accepting their history of mental illness. Information from third parties such as family, friends or past carers will always be important, and invaluable in circumstances where the client is unable to provide a clear history. Details of third party contacts such as telephone numbers, e-mail addresses and the relationship they have to the client should be carefully recorded, particularly as these details may be required should a crisis or change of situation occur. Depending on the nature of this information, consideration should be given to where third party information is recorded.

Some individuals may have a track record of early warning signs (see Chapter 1, Handout 1.5 Early warning signs), which might precede a deterioration in a person's mental health and any subsequent risk behaviours, and these should be carefully noted in addition to any known adverse reactions to particular events ('trigger factors') such as anniversaries, contact with certain people, seasons, or simply a lack of cigarettes. If these are known, they need to be clearly recorded.

Written records are an obviously valued source of information, but can be misleading, particularly where assessors have not had the opportunity to meet the individual for themselves. Occasionally, important risk factors may have been either minimized or omitted altogether from written reports.

Medication can play an extremely important role in risk management, and although drugs are far from being the sole focus of modern psychiatric treatment, a number of serious incidents have been preceded by failures of professionals to administer medications regularly, or through non-compliance with drugs such as anti-psychotics on the part of patients themselves (Hewlett 1998). For this reason it is important to determine not only what medications (if any) the person is taking, but what their attitudes and feelings are toward medication, and whether they suffer side-effects from all or any of the drugs they are prescribed. It is surprisingly common for patients to have little or no knowledge of the medications they are prescribed, or to have any idea how they work (Rogers *et al.* 1998). Lack of awareness and knowledge of prescribed medications is a key factor in non-compliance (Bagnall *et al.* 2003) and should therefore form a key part of the risk assessment, and help should be sought from the prescriber (usually either a psychiatrist or GP) or other mental health professional working with the client. Finally, the person's care plan should also include details of how medication should be administered and/or supervised.

Alcohol and other non-prescribed drugs

The link between substance misuse and mental illness has long been established as an important factor in risk assessment. A number of studies have shown that people with mental health problems are more likely to take drugs or drink heavily, and the risk of violence, suicide and self-neglect has been shown to increase markedly among mentally ill people who misuse substances (Soyka 2000).

Any risk assessment should routinely include an alcohol and drugs history, and where possible should be corroborated by third party sources. However, assessing an individual's relationship with non-prescribed drugs goes beyond how many cans of beer they drink or joints they smoke in the course of a day. The assessment also needs to determine how the person is affected by the substances they use, and attempt to find out *why* they use non-prescribed drugs. Of course, they may reply that they seek the same mix of relaxation, euphoria or simply having a good time as most other people who drink alcohol, snort cocaine or smoke cannabis, but often there are more complex factors involved (see Chapter 4 Working with Dual Diagnosis) and it is important that the assessment attempts to determine the relationship between a client's mental health, their use or misuse of drugs and any incidents of concern that have been associated with this relationship in the past or present.

Social support and relationships

Factors such as the symptoms or effects of mental illness can inform our assessment of risk, as does the effect of drugs and alcohol on any relevant situations or incidents that have happened in the past and are perhaps likely to happen again in the future. While these are essential elements to the overall assessment, the risks posed by one individual are unlikely to be influenced purely by internal factors such as low mood or, for example, a history of amphetamine abuse, but also by facets of the world around him or her that interact with their internal world to provoke anger, distress or violence.

A personal history is essential to an understanding of a client's situation. A key part of the assessment is determining what circumstances, events or relationships have been most important to that person, and how these have led them to be here talking to us. Conversation with a mental health care coordinator, family, carers or professionals who have known the individual previously will be invaluable, particularly where he or she has difficulty providing an account for themselves. An assessor may need to find out where a person has been living in recent years, and discover a little about their lifestyle, what they do for a living or how they occupy their time. Where key professionals or carers have been involved in the past, it is often a good idea to ask the subject of the assessment for permission to contact that worker for any further contribution they may be able to make in our assessment.

Where the person has been a hospital in-patient, an attempt should be made to speak to a mental health professional who has known them during this time. Even if a discharge summary has been provided, this will not necessarily include all incidents or situations that may have caused concern and may be repeated given a particular set of circumstances.

Some individuals may have lost touch with family, particularly where relationships in early life have been strained or even non-existent, but the assessment will benefit greatly from an exploration of the person's interaction with others, particularly where either past or current relationships have had some bearing on their mental health or, for example, a violent incident. Where family or social relationships are complex and have a direct bearing on the assessment of risk, it might be worth designing a 'genogram' (a diagrammatic representation of family and social relationships) with the client to highlight particular aspects of their history that may have caused difficulty or led to untoward situations or incidents.

Offending and aggression

It is important to note that risk assessment is a global process involving the identification of factors that may contribute to various forms of undesirable or dangerous events, and while criminal acts form only part of the overall risk profile, a history of offending is universally acknowledged as a key indicator of future offending and is an area that must be researched as part of our overall assessment (Monahan *et al.* 2001).

Where clients do have a history of offending it is important to have some form of chronological record of offences, and where gaps exist these should be clearly recorded along with reasons why the client's offending history is not fully comprehensive. It is not always the case that incidents of assault or aggression result in criminal conviction, particularly where the perpetrator has spent periods of time as a hospital in-patient or in supported accommodation (Miller and Maier 1987; Wright *et al.* 2002). For this reason it is important that we try to research and record any such incidents including, for example, attacks on staff or other clients or incidents of sexual harassment or assault. Sometimes even recorded offences will have little bearing on the nature of the incident itself. For example, an incident of fire setting may not always result in a charge of arson but may be reduced to criminal damage. Sex without consent may be considered as sexual assault rather than rape. While a list of recorded convictions may be of some use, assessments will benefit from a much greater understanding of the context and circumstances of a client's offending. Where an offending history exists, it is essential that at least some aspects of motives, victims, substance use and any other important factors are identified.

Individuals will often be (unsurprisingly) reluctant to discuss past criminal offences, but where appropriate (see Handout 3.2 Confidentiality) information may be sought from professionals who have prior acquaintance with the subject of the assessment.

Finally, it is also important to identify and recognize any existing legal restrictions or court orders (anti-social behaviour orders [ASBOs] or suspended sentences, for example) that may apply. This may not be divulged by the subject of the order, and may not be immediately obvious particularly where that person has moved from place to place or has led a chaotic lifestyle with little contact from health or social services workers.

Managing risk

By the end of the information collation stage, a large amount of data has been collated that will guide and inform a risk management plan. Whether this is a 'standalone' document or incorporated within a care plan, risk management should ideally be born of collaboration between the worker(s) who has carried out the initial assessment, their colleagues, other agencies involved in the care of the client, and of course the client him or herself. The regular CPA reviews convened by a client's care coordinator are an ideal forum to discuss risk management with the subject of the plan in a multi-disciplinary environment.

The process of devising a risk management strategy involves the processing of large amounts of information and using the key points to identify and manage key areas of risk. Readers of a culinary bent will be familiar with the process of 'reducing' a sauce, whereby a pan of liquid is slowly simmered until much of the liquid has evaporated and a thicker, more concentrated sauce is left. This is exactly what will happen with the collated information.

The assessment phase may have yielded a large volume of information, particularly in cases where the client has a long history of contact with mental health services and/or other agencies such as housing providers. Some of this information will prove vital in the management of any identified risks, while some may be interesting, but essentially superfluous to a simple, transparent risk management plan.

Having interviewed the client, and perhaps read reports and spoken to third parties, the assessor should now have a reasonably good idea of what risk factors exist, and how they interact. This information now needs to be condensed by reviewing the recorded information and picking out key points that will need to be addressed.

The final stage is to look at the risk factors with the client (if he or she is willing) and devise a strategy for managing risk that takes into account the potential hazards identified, a formulation of how these hazards interact with the person's past and current situation, and a list of actions to minimize the risks along with a clear identification of who is responsible for each action. It may be appropriate for a care plan or risk management strategy to highlight possible 'trigger factors' and offer a profile of early warning signs. A 'crisis plan' might also be required here, particularly if there is an identified likelihood of situations deteriorating over a short period of time. A crisis plan should include details of relevant contacts and clear instructions as to what needs to be done given a particular set of circumstances such as a client's unexplained disappearance, or the emergence of early warning signs. Finally, the simple mnemonic ORCAS (Ongoing, Reviewed, Communicated and Simple) (see Handout 3.3 ORCAS) is a useful means of remembering the most important principles of designing and implementing a risk management strategy.

References

Bagnall, A., James, L., Ginelly, L., Lewis, R., Glanvilles, J., Gilbody, S. *et al.* (2003) 'A systematic review of atypical antipsychotic drugs in schizophrenia.' *Health Technology Assessment 7*,13, http://www.ncchta.org/project.asp?PjtId=1235 (accessed on 22 February 2006).

Department of Health (1999) *Health Service Circular 1999/012: Caldicott Guardians.* London: Department of Health.

Hewlett, M. (1998) *Medication, Non-compliance and Mentally Disordered Offenders.* London: Zito Trust.

Miller, R. and Maier, G. (1987) 'Factors affecting the decision to prosecute mental patients for criminal behavior.' *Hospital and Community Psychiatry 38*, 1, 50–55.

Monahan, J. and Steadman, H., Silver, E., Applebaum, P.S., Robbins, P.C., Mulvey, E.P. (2001) *Rethinking Risk Assessment: The MacArthur Study of Mental Disorder and Violence.* New York: Oxford University Press.

Rogers, A., Day, J.C., Williams, B., Randall, F., Wood, P., Healy, D. and Bentall, R. (1998) 'The meaning and management of neuroleptic medication: a study of patients with a diagnosis of schizophrenia.' *Social Science Medicine 47*, 9, 1313–1323.

Sheppard, D. (1996) *Learning the Lessons.* London: Zito Trust.

Soyka, M. (2000) 'Substance misuse, psychiatric disorder and violent and disturbed behaviour.' *British Journal of Psychiatry 176*, 345–350.

Taylor, P. and Gunn, J. (1999) 'Homicides by people with mental illness: myth and reality.' *British Journal of Psychiatry 174*, 9–14.

Wright, S., Gray, R., Parkes, J. and Gournay, K. (2002) *The Recognition, Prevention and Therapeutic Management of Violence in Acute In-patient Psychiatry: A Literature Review and Evidence-based Recommendations for Good Practice.* London: United Kingdom Central Council for Nursing, Midwifery and Health Visiting.

Useful resources

Websites

Health and Safety Executive: www.hse.gov.uk

The National Confidential Inquiry into Suicide and Homicide by People with Mental Illness: www.national-confidential-inquiry.ac.uk

The Zito Trust: www.zitotrust.co.uk

Books

Kemshall, H. and Pritchard, J. (1995) *Good Practice in Risk Assessment and Risk Management.* London: Jessica Kingsley Publishers.

Moore, B. (1996) *Risk Assessment: Practitioner's Guide to Predicting Harmful Behaviour.* London: Whiting & Birch.

O'Rourke, M. and Bird, L. (2001) *Risk Management in Mental Health: A Practical Guide to Individual Care and Community Safety.* London: The Mental Health Foundation.

Prins, H. (2005) *Offenders, Deviants or Patients?* London: Routledge.

Case notes: Jenny

Jenny is 45 and has a 20-year history of schizophrenia. She is well known by the local CMHT and has been admitted to various hospitals a number of times following relapses of her psychotic illness. For most of her adult life she has slept rough, has drunk heavily and drifted from place to place. She has also engaged in prostitution to fund her drinking, which she claims is a far more effective anti-psychotic than the tablets her psychiatrist prescribes for her. She has been sexually assaulted a number of times, either while drunk or during periods of acute illness when she occasionally strips naked and claims to be an 'Earth Goddess'.

For the past year she has been living in a flat provided by a supported housing organization, which has allocated a keyworker who visits regularly to collect rent and offer support. She has a very good relationship with the keyworker, and has begun to attend a horticulture course at a local college. Jenny also visits a local mental health day centre, and has a community psychiatric nurse (who is also her care co-ordinator under the care programme approach) who convenes CPA reviews every six months and helps Jenny come to terms with her diagnosis of schizophrenia, and understand the effects of the anti-psychotic medication she is prescribed.

Jenny has no criminal record and denies ever having been violent toward others, but has tried to kill herself on several occasions over the last 20 years. Prior to moving into her new flat, Jenny had been admitted to hospital after an attempt to kill herself with a large overdose of paracetamol combined with several litres of strong cider. She reports that this was prompted by her becoming upset by beliefs that people were spreading rumours about her, namely that she was having sex with young boys. She was referred to the special needs housing association and discharged to her flat after several months in hospital, during which time she was treated with anti-psychotic medication and helped to learn more about her illness and the effect that alcohol has upon her.

Jenny's life has been remarkably stable for the last year. She has made friends locally, looks after her flat and her illness has been well controlled with medication. She has reduced her alcohol intake considerably, although she still binge drinks occasionally to cope with difficult life events. Jenny has no contact with family, although she had a baby 20 years ago who was given up for adoption. She has recently had some contact from social services informing her that her son is now trying to trace her and would like to meet her. Jenny remains ambivalent about this.

What are the 'risk factors'?

- Mental health: Jenny suffers from schizophrenia and has experienced frequent relapses that are often brought about by alcohol misuse. She is prescribed anti-psychotic medication, but has in the past failed to take this in the belief that alcohol is more effective in treating her symptoms.

✓

- Alcohol and other non-prescribed drugs: Jenny has a long history of alcohol abuse and she uses alcohol to 'self-medicate', although it appears to worsen her psychotic symptoms. She has reduced her alcohol intake since discharge from hospital, but still binge drinks when stressed.

- Social support and relationships: Jenny has no family but is otherwise well supported in the community. Previously she has slept rough and lived a chaotic existence. She has a son who wishes to make contact with her after being adopted as a baby.

- Offending and aggression: No history recorded or reported.

- Suicide and self-harm: Jenny has made several life-threatening suicide attempts. The last was three months ago using a large amount of paracetamol tablets combined with alcohol and preceded by paranoid delusional ideas.

- Other factors (1): Jenny has been left with quite extensive liver damage through a combination of long-term alcohol abuse and several overdose attempts. She has been warned that a further major overdose will prove almost certainly fatal.

- Other factors (2): Jenny is vulnerable to sexual exploitation and assault.

Conclusions

From even a relatively small amount of information a 'formulation' of the risks posed in this case can be devised. The risks fall into three main categories:

1. suicide
2. sexual assault/exploitation
3. self-neglect.

It is not possible to make any precise predictions as to whether these events will happen again or not, although the mental health team and the housing providers could minimize the risks by exerting a higher degree of support or even containment. However, Jenny now lives independently and enjoys a better quality of life than she has experienced for many years. A formulation of Jenny's situation and circumstances suggests some relationship between her mental health problems, alcohol abuse and the identified risk factors, although the exact dynamics of this relationship are still not entirely clear from the information available here. In the short

Jenny (continued)

term, a potential 'trigger factor' has been identified in the fact that her son wishes to make contact after being adopted as a baby, a situation that has the potential to upset Jenny.

Risk management

After careful consideration and discussion between Jenny, her housing association keyworker and her care coordinator, a care plan is produced that focuses upon the management of the substantial risks posed by Jenny to herself. The care plan identifies the potential hazards that may befall Jenny, and makes clear the need to minimize the potential for relapse into psychotic illness by providing ongoing social and professional support, helping Jenny cope with life stresses (such as her son's wish to make contact with her) without recourse to alcohol, and help her maintain compliance with the medication she is prescribed.

Jenny agrees that she will inform one of her care workers immediately should she feel tempted to attempt suicide, and she has consented to her care coordinator contacting her horticultural tutor to request that he alerts the CMHT should Jenny not attend as usual or present any cause for concern. Finally, the care coordinator will take a detailed look at Jenny's history and work with her to draw up a profile of early warning signs that might be recognized as indicators of her becoming unwell.

Ongoing risk management

The care plan and risk management strategy is constantly revised as circumstances change, and reviewed regularly at CPA meetings by those involved.

Jenny: points for reflection

1. Jenny prefers to 'self-medicate' with alcohol rather than taking prescribed medication. How does her alcohol abuse contribute to the overall risks involved?

2. Part of Jenny's risk management plan involves identification of 'early warning signs'? Can you suggest examples of what these might be?

3. Of the risk assessment and management factors outlined above, which are the most important in both the short and longer term?

✓

Handout 3.1 First contact

In some (but not all) situations, agencies or individual workers will be required to conduct a formal assessment process based on a referral from a third party organization. Examples might include the referral of a hospital patient to a specialist housing provider, or referral of a housing association tenant to day care services. Risk is not necessarily a concern at this stage, but there are several useful pointers toward a 'good practice' model for staff acquainting themselves with prospective service users.

The referral

A written or verbal referral should contain everything needed in order to offer an individual an appointment for assessment, although they can typically vary in quality from the highly detailed to the bare minimum, such as a name, a date of birth and an address.

The referrer should make clear that they have discussed this with the person concerned, and that they have given consent for their details to be shared with a third party. A 'usable' referral will also include at least a valid reason for the referral (including what it is that the client hopes to achieve with your service), and some background information including any relevant personal history and an account of the person's current mental health problems. The referrer should also draw attention to any current risk behaviours or other immediate concerns.

Assuming that some form of meeting will take place prior to any further action being taken, more information about the individual and their current circumstances may be sought before offering an appointment.

An invitation to meet

A letter or telephone call is likely to be the first contact with the person who has been referred. As well as informing them of the location and time of the appointment, it is important to make them aware of who will be present at the meeting, and why. Some contact details might also be provided should the appointment need to be changed.

The appointment

Most people feel a little uncomfortable meeting strangers, and an assessment interview is likely to be one of the less relaxed situations a prospective client will encounter. For this reason an initial meeting might ideally be carried out with the referrer present, or with someone known to the subject of the assessment. For workers carrying out an assessment interview, it may be helpful to be accompanied by a colleague who can not only supply an alternative viewpoint, but can also share note-taking or recording tasks. There are a number of other factors that need to be considered. First, the location of the meeting. The referral information and client's history should aid the decision, particularly with a view to any potential risks that may have been identified. If the person to be interviewed has a history of 'acting out' in stressful situations, we might wish the interview to take place in a safer environment than, for example, a home address.

There are a number of factors to consider when deciding on the time of the appointment. First, how long should the interview last? Consider that a brief ten-minute 'meet and greet' is hardly allowing for the forming of rapport or a detailed assessment of a person's suitability for a service, while a two-hour interview is likely to leave the interviewee (not to mention the assessor) feeling bored, irritable or restless.

We have already highlighted the potential stresses of such a situation, and our first task on meeting a prospective client is to try and put them at ease. If conducting an initial meeting with a colleague, a decision might be made beforehand as to who will 'take the lead' in the assessment, and respective roles should be explained to the interviewee beforehand. Confidentiality policies should be explained, and the subject of assessment reassured that information will be shared only with their consent and on a 'need to know' basis unless issues of public safety are raised.

The worker leading the assessment should check that the individual knows why they have been referred, and then explain the reason and purpose for the assessment. At the start of the assessment, it might also be wise to suggest that they request a break if at any time they feel the need.

If the person to be assessed appears to be under the influence of either drugs or alcohol, there is little likelihood of being able to form a rapport or to obtain a realistic picture of that person. In this instance it should be explained to the person that the assessment meeting will not go ahead, and another appointment made if this seems appropriate.

Handout 3.2 Confidentiality

One of the most frequently asked questions from mental health agencies such as housing providers concerns the question of referrers being unwilling to disclose sensitive information (such as criminal records) about clients. Whether this is born of a genuine concern to maintain client confidentiality, or is a more cynical ploy to successfully accommodate an otherwise 'difficult to place' individual, it is a constantly recurring problem.

The advent of community care has highlighted the issue of information sharing between health, social services and agencies such as providers of housing and day-care services. A lack of communication and a reluctance on the part of referrers to share important information regarding histories of violence and offending has been identified as a key factor in several inquiry reports into serious crimes perpetrated by mentally ill people.

Health and social services professionals are placed in the difficult position of being bound by professional codes of conduct that stress the importance of maintaining patient or client confidentiality, and seeking the express consent of the individual to reveal information about themselves to third parties. Unsurprisingly, those who have a criminal record may be unwilling for this information to be disclosed and may expressly forbid professionals from disclosing this to others.

On the other hand, most health and social care organizations have clearly defined policies and procedures on confidentiality. Most echo the general principle that maintaining confidentiality is paramount while making clear that where information directly concerns issues of public or client safety (for example, a history of assault or attempted suicide) then these facts warrant disclosure, albeit on a strictly 'need to know' basis. In cases where either referrers or care providers are unsure of whether or not to disclose information, or are concerned that key facts concerning risk have been withheld, it may be possible to seek the advice of a local 'Caldicott guardian' (see below) for further guidance.

Another key question that often causes confusion is when, or in what circumstances, information should be disclosed to the police. Again, local and organizational policies will mostly dictate good practice in this area, but as a rule of thumb the principle of public and client safety is an overarching guide. Assuming some form of crisis has occurred to warrant police involvement (such as a disappearance or a violent incident) carers might need to disclose whatever information is *essential* for officers to offer support and intervene.

Caldicott guardians

In 1997 the government appointed Dr Fiona Caldicott to investigate concerns around patient confidentiality raised by emerging methods of electronic record-keeping in health and social care. As a result of Dr Caldicott's report, all National Health Service trusts and local authority social services departments are now required to appoint a 'Caldicott guardian' (Department of Health 1999). Caldicott guardians are senior staff designated to protect patient or client information, and to provide guidance and strategic development (for example, the design of policies and procedures) around confidentiality. Each organization's Caldicott guardian is also responsible for ensuring that legislation such as the Data Protection Act (1998) and the Mental Health Act (1983) is adhered to by their organization's working practices.

✓

Handout 3.3 ORCAS (Ongoing, Reviewed, Communicated and Simple)

A simple mnemonic to outline the key principles of risk assessment and management:

Ongoing

Risk is a dynamic process and situations will change over time. Risk factors need to be continually monitored.

Reviewed

A risk management strategy warrants regular review involving both the client and all professionals and carers involved in his or her care. If meetings have been arranged, it is a care coordinator's responsibility to invite relevant parties to a meeting at a mutually convenient time at which attendance should be prioritized.

Communicated

Clear lines of communication between colleagues, clients and other key individuals are essential for effective risk management. Numerous inquiry reports have highlighted time after time how poor communication between agencies has led to serious incidents and, in some cases, death.

and
Simple

A risk management strategy is of little use if it looks like a wiring diagram, or is buried within a pile of notes in a cupboard. As a point of reference, the strategy should be easily comprehensible to anyone involved in the care of the client, from the care coordinator to a locum or agency housing worker.

Risk assessment and management

- Risk: the balance between the potential benefit of a proposed action and the potential harm that an action may cause.

- Good risk assessment enables informed decision making.

- Involves the identification of factors and circumstances that may contribute to an untoward incident.

- A dynamic and ongoing process that changes with time and circumstances.

- Information gathering covers the following areas:
    - personal history
    - mental health
    - substance misuse
    - social supports and relationships
    - history of offending and aggression.

- Information collated informs the risk management plan.

- ORCAS: Ongoing, Reviewed, Communicated and Simple.

Chapter 4

Working with Dual Diagnosis

The term 'dual diagnosis' refers to people who suffer from severe mental illness *and* have problems with drugs or alcohol to the extent that their mental and physical health is adversely affected and results in a complexity of mental health and social needs. As a substantial population, it is only relatively recently that the 'dually diagnosed' have been recognized as a unique client group with specific problems and challenges to mental health workers.

If dual diagnosis appears to be something of a new phenomenon, this is not because the mentally ill have only just begun to smoke cannabis or snort cocaine, but because the research-based recognition and definition of the problem (mainly from the United States) has only appeared in the literature during the last 15 years, and has been recognized in the United Kingdom even more recently.

One of the first studies to identify a link between substance misuse and mental illness was conducted in the United States (Regier *et al.* 1990). This was an 'epidemiological' study (or in other words, the scientific study of factors affecting the health and illness of individuals and populations) which examined the relationship between severe mental illness and substance misuse. The researchers found that almost half of those diagnosed with schizophrenia also had a substance misuse problem, with a similar number of bipolar disorder sufferers also being found to have a dual diagnosis. In the United Kingdom up to one-third of severely mentally ill patients known to mental health services also have substance misuse disorder, with cannabis and alcohol the most commonly used substances (Weaver *et al.* 2002).

A key problem with dual diagnosis is the confusion and lack of clarity about what the term actually means. Mental health professionals refer to dual diagnosis as a 'comorbidity' of problems, namely the combination of severe mental illness with a problematic use of drugs and/or alcohol. In this context, 'mental illness' usually refers to psychotic conditions such as schizophrenia, bipolar disorder or depression.

A substance misuse disorder does not necessarily imply 'dependence' or 'addiction', but defines a situation where a person's use of drugs or alcohol becomes problematic and seriously impairs their quality of life and ability to function as part of a community.

While dual diagnosis remains the most commonly used terminology in the United Kingdom, it is worth noting that 'comorbidity' and 'co-occurring addictive and mental disorder' (COAMD) are often-used terms elsewhere, particularly in the United States. Dual diagnosis is also used in the learning disability field to describe learning disabled people with a co-occurring mental illness.

Illegal drugs such as cannabis, ecstasy or amphetamines are enjoyed by a large section of the 'normal' population on a regular basis without any harmful effects on mental health, but for people with severe mental health problems the effects of these substances can be detrimental to both social functioning and long-term well-being. In this context, clinicians talk of 'misuse' of drugs or alcohol. This is because the substances are taken in quantities great enough to cause harm to the individual, which may be of a physical, psychological or social nature. For the person who suffers from severe mental illness, such harmful consequences are likely to already exist, and drinking and drug taking are therefore more likely to exacerbate these problems.

While the precise definition of dual diagnosis may appear a little problematic, there can be little doubt that this client group suffers a number of adverse consequences. Mental health workers will almost unanimously advise mentally ill people that substance use will exacerbate their symptoms. There is conclusive evidence that dual diagnosis clients suffer more severe psychotic symptoms, are admitted more frequently, and spend much longer periods in hospital than other people with histories of mental disorder (Weaver *et al.* 2002). Homeless people are particularly likely to have a mental illness combined with substance misuse problems (Warnes *et al.* 2003), and dual diagnosis is often associated with non-compliance with treatment and a tendency to drop out of contact with mental health services (Hunt, Bergen and Bashir 2002). Dually diagnosed people are also more susceptible to physical ill health (Strathdee *et al.* 2002).

A further difficulty facing the client with a dual diagnosis is the frequent failure of both mental health and substance misuse services to take responsibility for treating and supporting an individual. The latter may be unwilling to concede that the client's problems can be addressed until he or she has had treatment for their mental illness, while mental health services will often see drinking or drug taking as the 'primary' problem and may be reluctant to intervene until at least some degree of abstinence has been achieved (Rethink Dual Diagnosis Research Group 2004).

However, recent government initiatives and policy frameworks such as the Department of Health's good practice guide (Department of Health 2002) recommend the need for clear local policies for dual diagnosis, and place the initial onus of responsibility firmly at the feet of mental health services for assessing persons with mental illness and substance misuse problems. With the increasing realization that dual diagnosis represents a growing and specific problem in mental health care, local services are beginning to develop targeted strategies in accordance with the Department of Health guidelines. Dedicated dual diagnosis teams and individual workers are now being trained and deployed, particularly in urban communities where there is likely to be a greater concentration of mentally ill individuals with drug and alcohol problems.

Why do mentally ill people drink and take drugs?

The mentally ill often use substances for the same reasons as anyone else. In other words, they like to enjoy a drink or share a joint with friends and acquaintances. However, a significant body of individuals also have quite unique and specific reasons for using alcohol, cannabis or crack cocaine.

Self-medication

Many mentally ill people sometimes have more confidence in alcohol or cannabis than the often powerful combinations of drugs prescribed for them by a GP or psychiatrist. Non-prescribed drugs are completely within the control of the user, and should they decide to 'prescribe' themselves strong lager or a joint, this may be seen as preferable to having mental health professionals or carers telling them what to take, and when.

Professionals will normally assume that non-prescribed drugs are 'a bad thing', but it is difficult to ignore the fact that many clients see intoxication as a reliable means of getting rid of distressing voices, calming themselves down or simply cheering themselves up. Nonetheless, while smoking a joint may have an immediate and desirable effect for the individual, the longer-term risks of drug or alcohol are substantial in terms of worsening symptoms and a raised risk of self-harm or aggression (Soyka 2000).

'Dutch courage'

Anxiety and low self-esteem are common and often severe features of many mental disorders. Alcohol in particular is often cited by clients as a means by which they can participate in normal life without feeling 'paranoid' or afraid. In much the same way as many people will have a few drinks or an ecstasy tablet before a party or social event, some individuals with mental health problems may need some degree of intoxication just to be able to face a trip to the supermarket or to get to an appointment with their GP.

Normalization

One of the most devastating effects of mental illnesses such as schizophrenia is the destruction of the sufferer's personality and the subsequent inability to take part in a social life. Drug and alcohol use can be seen as a means of entry to social groups. While professionals will usually frown upon substance use, drug taking or drinking in a social context does represent some semblance of 'normality' for those who are often socially isolated by the stigma and debilitating effects of mental illness. Nonetheless, mental health workers may be familiar with the vulnerability and criminalization that are often associated with dual diagnosis (see Case notes: Wayne).

Escape

As well as being a means of recreation for millions of 'normal' people, drug and alcohol intoxication is often misleadingly seen as a means of 'anti-depressant', a view often endorsed by television dramas and movies showing characters 'drowning their sorrows' or obliterating painful memories or feelings through alcohol or cocaine. For those with mental health problems, feelings and memories are more likely to be painful or negative.

Mental illness is undoubtedly problematic, but does not in any way guarantee the sufferer a life of unremitting unhappiness. Nonetheless, a small group of those with severe and enduring mental health problems do become disengaged from family and friends, and even with the benefits of support and treatment from professionals and other carers, find life extraordinarily difficult without the opportunity to escape into the relative comfort of drug or alcohol intoxication.

Helping people with dual diagnosis

In addition to treating the symptoms of mental illness and encouraging clients to abstain or reduce their use of drugs or alcohol, the care of this client group is an all-encompassing 'holistic' process addressing the complexity of social and lifestyle problems that are likely to be encountered. With the wide variety of needs associated with dual diagnosis comes the realization that not every individual will benefit from a 'blanket approach' to care, and some service users will not wish to engage at all.

The intervention of health and social services professionals will in many cases be provided in partnership with the non-statutory agencies such as housing associations, homelessness services and day care providers. For example, supported housing may offer stability and insulation from some of the pressures that force many clients into substance misuse in the first place. For those who may have previously missed appointments through poor memory or lack of motivation, housing workers may prove key to helping clients engage more successfully with, for example, the community mental health team (CMHT). With an increased likelihood of psychotic relapse, physical health problems, social isolation and, in some cases, aggression and criminality, dual diagnosis is perhaps one of the less popular issues to be addressed by either state-provided or non-statutory agencies (Hawkings and Gilburt 2004).

Much of the difficulty in engaging and treating this client group comes from the reluctance or perceived inability of professionals and community care agencies to address the complex needs of individuals who are often labelled as 'chaotic' or 'difficult'.

Substance misuse services and mental health teams differ quite markedly in the way they work, and often have a very different 'culture' from one another. For example, addiction services may expect their clients to be 'partners' in their care, attend appointments at a fixed venue, identify characteristics about themselves that may have led to their problems, and maintain total abstinence. This represents a very different scenario from that of a schizophrenic, who is more likely to be treated as someone with a 'disease' or 'illness' and who may at times need a degree of coercion or even compulsion in order to maintain their mental health, abstinence from substance misuse and a reasonable quality of life.

People with a dual diagnosis are often difficult to engage and may benefit from an 'assertive outreach' model. Assertive outreach teams provide intensive community support for severely mentally ill people who are 'difficult to engage' in more traditional services. Assertive outreach clients have previously failed to keep in touch with mental health services, or have spent large amounts of time as hospital in-patients, due in part to non-compliance with medication and their unwillingness to engage with health care staff on a regular basis. Typically, the make-up of the team is similar to that of a community mental health team, namely a psychiatrist, social worker, community psychiatric nurses, occupational therapists and a number of other professionals and unqualified workers. However, the members of the assertive outreach team will usually work with much smaller caseloads than their CMHT equivalents, allowing a more intensive input than would normally be available. In addition to providing treatments for severe mental illnesses, assertive outreach teams focus on the basic needs of life such as shelter, nutrition and social and financial support. They also work hard to encourage clients to lead as 'normal' a life as possible, and by default will work with a group of people who have become significantly marginalized from mainstream society.

Assessment

There are several approaches to dual diagnosis that have been shown to promote recovery, lessen the likelihood of relapse and encourage a much improved quality of life. However, treatment or support will be of little benefit without the advantage of a thorough assessment beforehand. Of particular importance are the client's account of their drinking and/or drug taking, their history of mental health problems, and how the two interact. The person may or may not be physically dependent on non-prescribed drugs, but while a purely quantitative account (i.e. how much, what and when) of substance misuse is of obvious benefit, it is equally important to create a picture of *why* that individual uses or abuses substances. There are a range of possible explanations for problematic substance misuse among the mentally ill, some of which are 'generic' (common to substance misuse or dependence among the general population) and some, such as 'self-medication', that may be reasonably specific to the dual diagnosis population.

Assessors need to be mindful of the wide range of mental health problems experienced by the person (remembering that diagnoses often overlap and are of only partial help in understanding why a person behaves or thinks in a certain way) and the equally wide range of behaviours that might be labelled as 'substance misuse'. The individual may experience problems from only occasional use of, for example, cannabis, or may indulge in regular binge drinking once or twice a week, or may be physically dependent on crack cocaine. Clients or other sources of information may identify 'poly-drug' abuse, which is, as the name suggests, the taking of two or more different substances either simultaneously or at different times, sometimes according to availability.

The assessment needs to enable the assessor to obtain some idea of how an individual's life is directly or indirectly influenced by mental illness and substance use and to gain a perspective from the client how they might like to benefit from intervention, or even whether they wish us to intervene at all. However, it is important to remember that for some clients who are acutely ill it may not be possible to obtain this information at the initial assessment and their mental state may need to be stabilized before they are able to answer these questions.

What is certainly key to working with this client group is the workers' ability to foster non-judgemental client-centred rapport with individuals who are often vulnerable, chaotic and poorly motivated to receive help (Rethink Dual Diagnosis Research Group 2004). The workers' own attitudes to the clients' presenting problems will have an influence on the development of the rapport. The conflict for many workers is that mental illness is usually seen as something that 'happens' to those unfortunate enough to suffer from schizophrenia or bipolar disorder, whereas substance misuse is a deliberate act under the direct control of the individual and is often seen in a more pejorative light. This conflict may hamper an assessor's ability to be non-judgemental and client-centred.

Workers need to be clear, realistic and honest, with a minimum of jargon or unrealistic expectations. The workers' expectations need to be realistic rather than idealistic and acknowledge the fact that the help that is being offered may not always be attractive to the client. Sometimes the most that can be expected is that the initial contact may be enough to encourage a further appointment when the person feels ready to address their problems.

Engagement

Treatment (in the medical sense) will include pharmacological therapy such as anti-psychotic medication, and often an educational approach that attempts to enable the client to learn about their illness, how their medication works, and how substances such as alcohol and cannabis might impact on their mental illness symptoms.

Specialist substance misuse professionals, or clinicians who have been trained and recruited to work specifically with dual diagnosis, will use a variety of therapeutic techniques to address a person's problematic use of drugs and alcohol.

However, the interventions employed to treat dual diagnosis will typically be as varied as the problems encountered by individuals and the geographical location in which treatment takes place. A thorough assessment will guide clinicians as to the preferred treatment options available, and will depend on factors such as the severity of symptoms, the effect his or her substance misuse has on their mental health and social functioning (and vice versa), the current risk assessment and whether the person binges, uses occasionally or is physically dependent.

What is common to most approaches to dual diagnosis is the adoption of a 'collaborative approach'. By this we mean not only collaboration with other care workers and agencies, but the engagement of the client in a 'partnership' with professionals and carers, particularly where the person has had negative experiences of professional help in the past or has proved difficult to reach.

In most cases this may mean working within a mutually agreed framework and offering an approach that is focused on the needs of the client rather than those of the organization. Working with dual diagnosis clients can be a frustrating process, necessitating the setting of easily achievable goals and accepting that the pace of change may be slow, often with frequent setbacks and obstacles.

Initiating and maintaining some form of realistic and supportive relationship has been found to be one of the most effective factors in the overall care of mentally ill people who have drug and alcohol problems. In addition to using communication skills to form a rapport with new or prospective clients, offering assistance in some of the more basic needs such as housing, benefits advice, nutrition or taking medication will often offer an invaluable adjunct to treatment techniques employed by specialist clinicians. Motivational interviewing is a widespread and well-researched method of specialist intervention based on cognitive behaviour therapy (see Chapter 2 Treatment and Support), which offers a staged and highly structured one-to-one approach with clients over a series of sessions (Hawkings and Gilburt 2004).

It is unrealistic to expect any immediate change in an individual's lifestyle or substance misuse habits. The problems the dually diagnosed client presents with will have developed over a period of years so it is important to remember that change is a long and slow process and it is realistic to expect lapses into past behaviours and coping strategies along the way. As a worker it is important that a working, non-judgemental rapport has been established before beginning to suggest any significant change, or discussing longer-term treatment options.

For the dually diagnosed client it is essential that clear boundaries are established from the beginning (for example, in the provision of supported accommodation). The boundaries will need clear explanation along with an unambiguous account of why those boundaries exist and consequences if the boundaries are broken.

The dual diagnosis toolkit

This client group present a considerable degree of challenge to both health professionals and non-statutory services. Dually diagnosed individuals tend to suffer more severe symptoms of mental illness, are more socially disabled, and often present as vulnerable and chaotic. They often have quite unique and understandable reasons for heavy drinking or drug taking, but are seldom self-motivated to cease or reduce their use of non-prescribed drugs. As if this were not enough to dissuade the prospective care worker or health professional, dual diagnosis is more likely than other disorders to be at the root of violence and hostility. While expectations of effecting lasting change may appear limited, the very high prevalence of dual diagnosis means mental health workers are increasingly likely to encounter individuals who are beset by both mental illness and substance misuse problems.

A client-centred and collaborative approach, combined with the provision of comprehensive assessment and the meeting of basic needs, can achieve positive results (see Case notes: Wayne). The 'toolkit' is designed as an *aide-mémoire* for workers, introducing some of the key skills and attitudes that will help mental health carers work with dually diagnosed clients.

The pragmatist

Care workers of any discipline would be hard pressed to suggest that they did not rate the desire to 'help people' as a key motivation for doing their job. Dual diagnosis can severely test this notion, and it is the pragmatist who is able to be *realistic* as opposed to optimistic. Simply being able to maintain contact with individuals can, in many cases, be considered a major achievement where non-compliance and 'disappearance' are frequent problems in trying to achieve at least a basic quality of life for the client.

The analyst

The analyst is not content with the information that 'Client X' is a 'heavy drinker'. The analyst is able to determine:

- what the substance of abuse is, and how much is being consumed

- what the circumstances of the client's abuse are

- what effect alcohol or drugs has on mental state

- whether this combination leads to significant problems for the client or others

- why the client needs to drink or ingest drugs.

The fence-maker

Many community resources are governed by a clear 'dry house' policy. The fence-maker must be adept at ensuring clear boundaries are set and maintained. This can be done without forcing the client to withdraw from whatever treatment plans have been set up. 'Therapeutic confrontation' is perhaps one of the key skills in working with the disorganization, vulnerability and disability often presented by dual diagnosis.

The motivator

Even when we are able to help the dual diagnosis client reduce harmful behaviour, what replaces that harmful behaviour? The motivator has the patience and interpersonal skills to help clients 'fill the gap' that was previously filled by substance use, and may come in the form of a structured activity. It is important that activities are achievable, realistic and do not set up the person for failure.

References

Department of Health (2002) *Mental Health Policy Implementation Guide: Dual Diagnosis Good Practice Guide.* London: Department of Health.

Hawkings, C. and Gilburt, H. (2004) *Dual Diagnosis Toolkit: Mental Health and Substance Misuse.* London: Rethink.

Hunt, G., Bergen, J. and Bashir, M. (2002) 'Medication compliance and comorbid substance abuse in schizophrenia: impact on community survival 4 years after a relapse.' *Schizophrenia Research 54,* 253–264.

Regier, D.A., Farmer, M.E., Rae, D.S., Loche, B.Z., Keith, S.J., Judd, L.L. and Goodwin, F.K. (1990) 'Co-morbidity of mental disorder with alcohol drug abuse: results from an epidemiological catchment area (ECA) study.' *Journal of the American Medical Association 264,* 2511–2518.

Rethink Dual Diagnosis Research Group (2004) *Living with Severe Mental Health and Substance Use Problems.* London: Rethink/Adfam.

Soyka, M. (2000) 'Substance misuse, psychiatric disorder and violent and disturbed behaviour.' *British Journal of Psychiatry 176,* 345–350.

Strathdee, G., Manning, V., Best, D., Keaney, F., Bhui, K., Wilton, J. *et al.* (2002) *Dual Diagnosis in a Primary Care Group (PCG): A Step-by-step Epidemiological Needs Assessment and Design of a Training and Service Response Model.* London: Department of Health.

Warnes, W., Crane, M., Whitehead, W. and Fu, R. (2003) *Homelessness Factfile.* London: Crisis.

Weaver, T., Charles, V., Madden, P. and Renton, A. (2002) *Co-morbidity of Substance Misuse and Mental Illness Collaborative Study (COSMIC).* London: Department of Health.

Useful resources
Websites

Alcohol Concern: www.alcoholconcern.org.uk

Drugscope: www.drugscope.org.uk

Homelesspages: www.homelesspages.org.uk

The Dual Diagnosis Information Project/Royal College of Psychiatrists: www.rcpsych.ac.uk/cru/complete/ddip.htm

Books and film

Dennison, S. (2003) *Handbook of the Dually Diagnosed Patient.* Philadelphia: Lippincott Williams and Wilkins.

Miller, W. and Rollnick, S. (2002) *Motivational Interviewing: Preparing People for Change.* New York: Guilford Publications.

Mind in Croydon (2004) *Pillar to Post – A Film About Dual Diagnosis.* London: Mind Publications.

Case notes: Wayne

Wayne is 25 years old. He has had a number of admissions to hospital and has recently been diagnosed with schizophrenia. As a child Wayne was overactive, and had difficulty concentrating in school, with teachers describing his behaviour as reckless and disruptive.

When Wayne started secondary school he began getting into trouble for fighting. His attendance became poor and he would often be awake until the early hours of the morning playing music and shouting out obscenities.

At the age of 14 Wayne was permanently excluded from school for seriously assaulting another pupil. He was seen by a child psychiatrist who formed the opinion that Wayne had a conduct disorder. Home tuition was arranged but was unsuccessful because of his hostility and poor motivation.

Wayne's parents began to notice that Wayne spent more and more time in his room with the curtains drawn and playing the same CD over and over again. He had by this time neglected what few interests he had previously enjoyed, such as supporting his local football team. His parents explained this as 'normal teenage behaviour'.

By the age of 17 Wayne had stopped leaving the house during the day. At night he went out only to return drunk, and was often irritable and aggressive. One evening while Wayne was out, his mother went into his room to collect his dirty clothes. In the pocket of a pair of trousers she found a bag containing cannabis. When Wayne returned home his parents confronted him, and he admitted to smoking cannabis on a regular basis. He told his parents that the FBI were following him and this was why he could only go out at night. His parents persuaded Wayne to see his GP. Wayne said he was frightened and asked his mother to go with him. He insisted on taking a blanket with him which he placed over his head. The GP recommended that Wayne see a drugs counsellor.

Wayne went to see the counsellor, but refused to answer certain questions. The counsellor decided that as Wayne was using cannabis and did not want to give up, there was little in the form of treatment to be offered.

Wayne began refusing to eat the food his mother cooked, but instead would get up in the middle of the night and prepare his own meals, often leaving the gas cooker on and the kitchen in chaos.

One night when Wayne was 18 his parents returned home to find all of the doors to the house locked and bolted with Wayne inside the house. He refused to let his parents in, saying that they were part of an FBI operation to have him assassinated. Not knowing what else to do Wayne's father called the police. After several hours of negotiations Wayne eventually opened the door, and he was taken into police custody. He was then assessed by a psychiatrist who agreed to admit him to hospital for assessment under the Mental Health Act. The police decided not to charge Wayne with any offence and his parents did not wish to press charges.

On admission to hospital, Wayne told the nursing staff that he had been drinking heavily and smoking cannabis in addition to using large amounts of amphetamines to make himself 'feel happier'. The results of a routine urine drugs screen confirmed that Wayne had been using both amphetamines and cannabis. Wayne did not tell the staff of the FBI plot to have him assassinated, nor of the hostile and abusive voices he heard in his head.

After a week in hospital Wayne was diagnosed with a drug-induced psychosis and discharged with an appointment to see the consultant psychiatrist in a month's time. Wayne did not attend this appointment, and his parents were not interviewed by any members of the multi-disciplinary team.

A number of brief hospital admissions followed due to Wayne having taken overdoses. They usually resulted in Wayne discharging himself or being discharged because he had assaulted staff or had been found drinking or smoking cannabis on the ward. Wayne always told the staff that he was using large amounts of drugs. Staff accepted this explanation but did not carry out urine drug screens to check. He was diagnosed as having a personality disorder and substance misuse disorder.

The situation at home became worse and Wayne's parents felt increasingly unable to cope. Wayne was hostile towards them, demanding money and using it to buy drugs. The final straw came when he threatened his father with a knife, and they decided that Wayne would have to move out. The incident was not reported to the police.

Wayne's mother found him a flat nearby, and as Wayne had no income his parents paid his rent. Wayne's father did not visit but his mother took him in a meal twice a day. She noticed that the curtains were always drawn and that Wayne had covered the windows with newspapers. The television was turned around so that the screen faced the wall. When she asked Wayne about this he told her that it was so he 'could not be watched'.

Wayne's mother went to see her GP and discussed her concerns with him. Wayne had lost weight, and he had stopped eating the food she took him. He was refusing to answer the telephone and would only let her into the flat if she used a password that he changed every visit and gave to her when she left. When she entered the flat Wayne insisted on searching her, and told her that this was in case she had been bugged. On one occasion he had ripped the heels off her shoes in an attempt to check for hidden microphones.

The GP contacted the local community mental health team (CMHT) and requested an urgent assessment of Wayne. Following a detailed assessment he was admitted to the local psychiatric unit under the Mental Health Act. A routine drugs screen that had been done on the evening of Wayne's admission came back negative for all substances, although he insisted that he had been taking large amounts of substances both on the day of his admission and in the days leading up to it.

Wayne (continued)

Wayne was often observed shouting when he was alone, and he isolated himself. He had lost a large amount of weight from when he had not been eating and at first he refused to eat the hospital food. He wanted to sleep during the day and be up all night. Wayne was prescribed an atypical anti-psychotic and began a low key occupational therapy programme, which increased as his mental state improved.

Gradually Wayne began to tell a particular nurse of the voices he heard in his head telling him he would be killed, and that the FBI watched him through the television and knew his every move. He began eating again, and the nurse began talking to Wayne about his substance misuse. Both of Wayne's parents were interviewed and the full extent of his history became known.

Six months after his admission Wayne was diagnosed with schizophrenia, but had benefited from the treatment and support he had been given and was considered ready for discharge. During his time in hospital Wayne had learnt a lot about his illness and substance misuse problems, but the team felt he would need a high level of support in the community if he was to maintain this improvement, and his parents felt unable to have him home to live despite his recent progress.

Wayne was referred to and accepted by a fully staffed hostel with 24-hour support. He was given leave from his Mental Health Act section which meant that if his mental state deteriorated he could be returned to hospital and quickly treated. He was offered a daily programme of activities which he agreed to attend, and he began to see a worker from the local substance misuse service as well as having regular visits from a community psychiatric nurse (CPN).

At the hostel Wayne had a designated keyworker whom he learnt to trust. Initially the hostel staff dispensed his medication and helped Wayne attend his activity programme. His keyworker encouraged him to join the local gym and Wayne took part in social outings. Wayne was reminded to keep his outpatient appointments with health care professionals and agreed to sign an abstinence agreement, which meant if he used drugs or alcohol he could be asked to leave the hostel.

A few weeks after arriving at the hostel a change in Wayne's behaviour had been noticed. He had become secretive and irritable, and during a routine health and safety check staff discovered empty alcohol bottles under his bed together with a collection of prescribed medication that he had not taken. Wayne's CPN was contacted and the decision made that he should return to hospital. A drugs screen carried out on the day of his admission came back positive for cannabis. Following a further two weeks in hospital Wayne returned to the hostel. He received a written warning for having alcohol in his room.

Wayne's CPN visited regularly and worked closely with the hostel staff. Initially Wayne had needed reminding to take his medication, get up for meals and to attend his daily programme and social activities, but over the following months it was noticed that he was becoming increasingly independent, and with the support of the hostel staff began a self-medication programme. Wayne bought himself a mountain bike on which he went out accompanied by a member of staff. He also took up fishing and renewed his interest in his local football team.

The present: Wayne's Account

'I haven't touched anything for over a year now – not so much as a draw on a spliff. I really like it here but the first few weeks were a bit weird, and I thought a few puffs and a beer wouldn't do any harm and would do me more good than the tablets. But getting ill again and getting a written warning really scared me. I feel great now and I'm not under a section anymore, but that doesn't mean I'm not still tempted anymore or that I love taking the medication they give me. But that's life I suppose.

At the last review meeting they held, me and my keyworker thought it was about time I was moving on from here to a 'supported flat', but I still needed a bit of help staying well and keeping out of trouble. So the CPN and my keyworker will still keep in touch, and I still have to see the psychiatrist every now and then along with the drugs counsellor, who has really helped me find out why I was having to get wrecked all the time and helps me stay on the straight and narrow. I'm at college now doing musical technology, and I've made a few friends here and there who aren't into drugs or anything, so it will be great to have my own place and not have to share a bathroom or kitchen, but I'll definitely carry on fishing and biking, and getting along to as many home games as I can. I've even persuaded dad to start coming to football again!'

What changed for Wayne?

- A comprehensive assessment of his mental health and addiction problems that included gathering a detailed history from his family.

- With the use of routine drug screens, mental health professionals were able to establish the contribution Wayne's substance misuse made to his mental health problems.

- The correct diagnosis and treatment.

- Education about his illness and substance misuse helped Wayne to understand and manage his illness better.

- The provision of structure to Wayne's day.

✓

Wayne (continued)

- The structure and stability provided by the hostel and its staff in helping him to return to a normal lifestyle.

- The firm boundaries the hostel provided, such as signing an abstinence agreement and receiving a written warning when this was breached.

- The close working relationship between the hostel and the health care professionals involved.

Wayne: points for reflection

1. What are the early indicators that might distinguish Wayne's mental illness from 'normal teenage behaviour' as described by his mother?

2. Why might Wayne feel that cannabis and amphetamines are helpful to him?

3. When Wayne first comes into contact with mental health professionals there appears to be some confusion about diagnosis, and a reluctance to engage with him. Why might this be?

4. Which factors have been helpful in Wayne's progress of late?

5. How might housing and statutory staff (e.g. his CPN) best respond should Wayne return to substance misuse in the future?

Dual diagnosis difficulties

- a combination of severe mental illness and problems with drugs or alcohol
- one-third also have substance misuse problems
- adverse effects on mental and physical health
- complexity of mental health and social needs
- high rate of non-compliance with treatment
- confusion of responsibility between substance misuse services and mental health services.

Why do mentally ill people drink and take drugs?

- self-medication
- 'Dutch courage'
- normalization
- escape.

✓

Helping people with dual diagnosis

- a holistic approach; for example, symptoms, lifestyle, physical/mental health, accommodation etc.

- major emphasis on non-statutory services; for example, housing, day care

- many dually diagnosed clients difficult to engage: rapport building essential.

Assessment

- substance misuse: how much?

- what?

- in what circumstances?

- interaction with mental health

- use or abuse?

- non-judgemental, positive attitude required!

Engagement

- treatment of mental illness

- collaboration with other professionals/agencies

- specialist techniques; for example, motivational interviewing

- clear boundaries

- realistic expectations.

Chapter 5

Working with Personality Disorder

Personality disorder is not an illness or disease, but is a condition whereby a person's personality – that is, their mode of thinking, feeling and behaving – has become deeply problematic for both themselves and those around them. Whereas an illness such as schizophrenia or appendicitis are usually thought of as having certain key symptoms, personality disorder might be better described as a range of abnormal personality 'traits' that characterize how an individual acts and feels. In fact, some would argue that personality disorder is not so much a medical condition as a social problem. Its causes are more often attributed to developmental issues rather than any clear organic process and its status as a psychiatric disorder is often considered to be problematic (see Handout 5.4 PD or not PD?).

Whatever the arguments surrounding its validity as a bona fide mental disorder, personality disorder is defined and described as such by both major systems of disease recognition (see Chapter 1, Handout 1.1 Measuring mental health).

Using these widely accepted standards, studies have shown personality disorder to be surprisingly common in the general population, with at least one in ten people meeting the diagnostic criteria (de Girolamo and Dotto 2000), although only a relatively small number of these individuals will come to the attention of mental health services.

However, personality disorder has been shown to be particularly prevalent among certain groups. Studies among clients of drug and alcohol dependency services (Weaver *et al.* 2002), and surveys of prisoner populations (Singleton *et al.* 1998), suggest that substantial proportions of both these groups meet the diagnostic criteria. However, widespread and complex patterns of both personality disorder and other mental health problems in these groups often serve to create a somewhat chaotic scenario in which any strictly medical diagnosis, particularly one as difficult to recognize as personality disorder, remains largely invisible against a backdrop of crisis and catastrophic life events, making recognition and access to treatment yet more difficult.

Regardless of whether personality disorder becomes a medical problem, is part of a person's everyday life, or leads to imprisonment or substance dependence, it is invariably associated with failed and fractured relationships, difficulty forming close bonds with others and the potential to create considerable distress to both the affected individual and those around them.

However, despite the pessimism that often surrounds this condition, there is increasing evidence that a number of options for the care, support and treatment of this client group can prove helpful and effective in a variety of settings (National Institute for Mental Health in England 2003).

This chapter will look at some of the most common features of personality disorder, and suggest some useful ways of working with people who present services with some of their most difficult challenges.

What is personality disorder?

Clear signs of impending personality disorder will often have been evident since childhood, often associated with a history of neglect and trauma in early life. Personality disorder has a gradual onset and is persistent throughout the person's life. In other words it does not 'appear' in adulthood in the same way as bipolar disorder or schizophrenia. And whereas most forms of mental illness can now be attributed to malfunctioning brain receptors and neurotransmitters, researchers are yet to determine any such organic origins for personality disorder. There is certainly no such thing as an 'anti-personality disorder' drug.

Personality disorder is usually associated with deviant, anti-social or aggressive behaviour, often resulting in crisis, hospital admissions or imprisonment (see Handout 5.3 Personality disorder and the Mental Health Act). However, it has also been suggested that a number of successful people, from politicians, world leaders and business people to actors, rock stars and artists, have an otherwise undiagnosed personality disorder, and that the characteristics of an unstable and volatile personality that might otherwise have led to catastrophe have contributed to success, notoriety or both (Hare 1999).

Nonetheless, for the majority of mental health workers, personality disorder means a range of behaviours that invariably present challenges and difficulties to staff, other clients and the individual themselves. There are several different profiles of personality disorder, which often overlap with one another (see Handout 5.1 What's in a name?), but manipulation of others, aggressive and threatening behaviour, unreliability and challenges to perceived authority and the testing of rules and boundaries are all common features.

Personality disordered individuals have little ability to control impulses, with a low frustration tolerance and a tendency toward bouts of substance abuse or self-harm. They have a tendency towards 'all or nothing' thinking, whereby people or situations are seen as either very good or very bad, with little room for 'in betweens', and tend to be highly 'egocentric' with little or no thought for the needs or feelings of others. They often fail to learn by experience and continue to make the same mistakes over and over again, even when their actions lead to untoward circumstances or personal hardship. Unsurprisingly, people with personality disorder are seldom popular with others and tend to have few genuine friends or close bonds with others. While they can often be superficially charming and humorous, relationships are more likely to be based on instrumental gain rather than the warmth or affection upon which most people would base personal friendships and romantic attachments.

What causes personality disorder?

Research into the causes of personality disorder has yet to reveal a clear-cut 'aetiology' for the condition. Most mental health staff who have worked with personality disordered people will be familiar with histories of erratic parenting, childhood trauma and neglect. But growing up within a dysfunctional or abusive background is too simplistic an explanation, and does not explain why siblings from the same family, with similar if not identical backgrounds, often follow very different paths into adulthood, with perhaps one brother or sister developing personality disorder in adulthood while others go on to lead reasonably normal, happy lives. Where one or both parents have shown signs of personality disorder themselves, the question arises as to the relative impact of genetic heredity on their children. In the absence of large-scale twin studies, it is difficult (if not impossible) to separate out the influence of genetic heredity from poor parenting in the development of this disorder.

A further research complication is the heterogeneity of the disorder, or in other words, the high degree of overlap that exists between one type of personality disorder and another. To further complicate matters, other mental disorders (including, in many cases, dependence on drugs or alcohol) often exist 'comorbidly' with personality disorder.

While the relative importance of childhood development and upbringing is undisputed, the contribution of genetic and organic factors is emerging as an increasingly important area of research. A recent study among young children has highlighted the important role of genetic heredity in the development of some traits associated with future personality disorder, while other anti-social traits were found to have been influenced more by their developmental environment than genes alone (Viding *et al.* 2005).

It would seem likely that genetic inheritance does indeed play an important role in determining the *potential* for developing personality disorder, but environmental influences determine whether this genetic potential remains latent, or is 'switched on' by, for example, trauma or neglect in early life.

A diagnosis of exclusion?

With attributes such as these, and the fact that personality disorder is often combined with other 'comorbid' mental health problems such as substance dependence or depression, it is unsurprising that this is such an unpopular condition with both community workers and mental health professionals. The personality disordered are a population often excluded by services on the grounds that they tend to exhaust both individual workers and the teams with which they work. The effectiveness of hospital in-patient treatment is seen as debatable at best, with only crisis intervention or treatment of comorbid symptoms such as low mood or anxiety being offered as a realistic option by most acute in-patient units, and personality disordered patients often demanding staff resources grossly out of proportion to their numerical presence. Special hospitals and secure units specializing in the treatment of violent and offender patients provide care for a significant number of personality disordered individuals. Although most of this group will be detained under the Mental Health Act (see Appendix: Introducing the Mental Health Act 1983) there remains considerable disparity between individual services as to the treatability or otherwise of personality disordered patients (Beck-Sander and Kinsella 1998).

Of the treatment interventions indicated for personality disorder (see Handout 5.2 Treating personality disorder) few have been well researched and all require specialized resources and training (National Institute for Mental Health in England 2003). Psychological therapies are also heavily dependent on the full cooperation of the client, which is often not the case even when resources have been identified and referrals made. However, this does not mean that positive outcomes cannot be achieved, particularly within community environments and longer-term placements such as supported housing, where for many individuals, stability and relationship-building will begin to replace chaos and isolation, in many cases for the first time in an eventful and turbulent life.

The personality disorder toolkit

Personality disordered clients of health, social and non-statutory services are almost universally unpopular with workers. Faced with an array of complex needs, challenging situations and sometimes threatening and dangerous behaviours, it is little wonder that staff are often left feeling helpless, de-skilled and, in some cases, 'burnt out'. The personality disorder toolkit is simply an array of roles, tips and techniques that can be used in day-to-day practice with difficult situations and individuals. None of these tools are instant panaceas or 'magic wands', but used consistently over a period of time within a stable environment and with adequate support and supervision from colleagues, the toolkit is certainly a means of addressing some of the more problematic behaviours encountered with this client group.

The fence-maker

Personality disordered clients will often have little conception of the social norms that others might take for granted. The setting of clear boundaries is important for both worker and client so that both parties know 'where they stand'. Rules and boundaries are important but it is essential that there are good reasons for their existence, which should be explained clearly and unambiguously. It is also important that there is consistency within the staff group. If boundaries are interpreted differently between one staff member and another this can lead to confusion and ambiguity, a situation that may well be exploited by the client, leading to further confusion and confrontation.

The director

One of the key features of personality disorder is the individual's inclination towards impulsivity, having a tendency to react to situations without pausing for thought or consideration of consequences. The director seeks to help the person find alternative strategies to problems (whether real or perceived) and points out how past or present reactions might have led to further problems, whereas a little contemplation and insight might have led to a much improved outcome. Where personality disordered people often 'act out' their frustration in anti-social or aggressive ways, the director might also be able to help clients 'play back' their responses to difficult situations, and realize how their behaviour has affected both themselves and others.

The detective

Another key feature of this disorder is 'black and white thinking', or in other words taking the view of situations or people being either 'very good' or 'very bad' with little or no 'medium'. The detective encourages the client to 'test the evidence' before coming to extreme conclusions, and suggests they try to see the 'bigger picture' of a scenario.

The telescope

The telescope is all about making small, distant objects appear much closer. Personality disordered people often have little ability to identify their feelings or process emotions in the same way as most people. When asked how they feel, a typical response might be 'Don't know' or they might query the relevance of the question. The telescope monitors non-verbal cues and points these out, albeit with tact and a non-judgemental approach. A response such as 'You're looking a little miserable today' might lead to further exploration of why the person appears the way they do, particularly where the worker has an established rapport with the client and knows enough about their circumstances and behaviour to be able to draw out more expression and insight from that person than might otherwise be possible.

The straight bat

The straight bat represents a straightforward personal style as a response to clients who might be distrustful and manipulative in an attempt to maintain some semblance of order and control in an otherwise chaotic life. The straight bat presents a positive role model and takes a calm but robust stance to anti-social or threatening behaviours. Whereas it is sometimes tempting and all too easy for workers to become drawn into crises or problematic situations, the straight bat remains objective and tries to help the person resolve problems themselves while remaining 'off stage' themselves.

A further part of the role involves honesty. It is surprisingly (but understandably) common for staff to tell 'white lies' or withhold information in order to avert a crisis or to prevent the client 'acting out', perhaps in response to bad news. The short-term gains of such action are seldom rewarded by longer-term progress, and frequently leads to further conflict and an opportunity for personality disordered clients to cause conflict within a staff group.

The forcefield

Working in mental health is as different from working in a shop or an office as playing football in a back garden is from appearing in an FA Cup Final. Staff invest a considerable part of themselves, their own lives and their own personalities into the work they do, and nowhere is this more true than working with personality disorder. The development of a rapport with a damaged, distrustful person who has spent many years unable to form meaningful relationships with others can be ultimately rewarding. However, it is not uncommon for workers to allow personal and professional boundaries to become blurred, often with the effect of a parent/child scenario developing. The forcefield is about clarifying these personal/professional boundaries from the outset, and defining relationship expectations at an early stage. If clients are to be helped to develop their own coping and problem-solving skills for the future, staff members need to avoid the temptation to become over-involved, while encouraging the individual to address their own problems, albeit with sound advice and encouragement. The forcefield is also aware of the crucial importance of supervision from peers and managers, whether on a formal or 'ad hoc' basis.

The ray of light

The ray of light is aware that even the most difficult clients are also capable of being genuinely likeable, humorous and, in some cases, talented people. These attributes can be highlighted and encouraged. However, for many individuals with personality disorder, a life of chaos and unhappiness is familiar and comforting. Making progress and moving forward may often be interspersed with periods of unease and uncertainty. The ray of light is aware of this, and even anticipates and is prepared for occasional retreats into the 'comfort zone' by way of a return to familiar behaviours and attitudes. Many workers respond with disappointment when this happens. 'Just when we thought we were getting somewhere' is a familiar phrase in this scenario, but the ray of light remains optimistic, does not panic and continues using the array of tools outlined here. Pragmatism sometimes dictates that the client is not yet ready for permanent change, but often 'relapse' is short-lived and can be seen as a valuable learning experience.

References

American Psychiatric Association (2000) *Diagnostic and Statistical Manual of Mental Disorders, Fourth Edition.* Washington, DC: American Psychiatric Association.

Bateman, A. and Tyrer, P. (2002) *Effective Management of Personality Disorder.* London: National Institute for Mental Health in England.

Beck-Sander, A. and Kinsella, C. (1998) 'Patient selection and management in medium and low security hospitals.' *Psychiatric Care 5,* 3, 86–88, 90–91.

de Girolamo, G. and Dotto, P. (2000) 'Epidemiology of personality disorders.' In M.G. Gelder, J.J. Lopez-Ibor and N.C. Andreasen (eds) *New Oxford Textbook of Psychiatry, vol. 1.* Oxford: Oxford University Press.

Department of Health/Home Office (1999) *Managing Dangerous People with Severe Personality Disorder.* London: Home Office.

Dolan, B., Warren, F. and Norton, K. (1997) 'Change in borderline symptoms one year after therapeutic community treatment for severe personality disorder.' *British Journal of Psychiatry 171,* 274–279.

Hare, R. (1999) *Without Conscience.* New York: Guilford Publications.

Lees, J., Manning, N. and Rawlings, B. (1999) *Therapeutic Community Effectiveness: A Systematic International Review of Therapeutic Community Treatment for People with Personality Disorders and Mentally Disordered Offenders.* York: NHS Centre for Reviews and Dissemination, University of York (CRD Report 17).

National Institute for Mental Health in England (2003) *Personality Disorder: No Longer a Diagnosis of Exclusion.* London: Department of Health.

Office for National Statistics (2005) *Inpatients Formally Detained in Hospitals Under the Mental Health Act 1983 and Other Legislation.* Leeds: Health and Social Care Information Centre.

Rutter, D. and Tyrer, P. (2003) 'The value of therapeutic communities in the treatment of personality disorder: A suitable place for treatment?' *Journal of Psychiatric Practice 9,* 4, 291–302.

Singleton, N., Meltzer, H., Gatward, R., Coid, J. and Deasy, D. (1998) *Psychiatric Morbidity Among Prisoners in England and Wales.* London: Office for National Statistics.

Viding, E., Blair, J., Moffitt, T.E. and Plomin, R. (2005) 'Evidence for substantial genetic risk for psychopathy in 7-year-olds.' *Journal of Child Psychology and Psychiatry 46,* 6, 592–597.

Weaver, T., Charles, V., Madden, P. and Renton, A. (2002) *Co-morbidity of Substance Misuse and Mental Illness Collaborative Study (COSMIC).* London: Department of Health.

World Health Organization (1992) 'Classification of mental and behavioural disorders.' In *ICD-10.* Geneva: World Health Organization.

Useful resources

Websites

National Institute for Mental Health in England: www.nimhe.org.uk

The Home Office: Dangerous and Severe Personality Disorder: www.dspdprogramme.gov.uk

The Institute of Mental Health Act Practitioners: www.markwalton.net/sevpersdis.asp

Books

Cleckley, H. (1976) *The Mask of Sanity (Fifth Edition)*. St Louis: C.V. Mosby.

Kinsella, C. and Hannell, S. (2001) *Working with Personality Disorder*. Southampton: ROCC.

Masters, B. (1985) *Killing for Company*. London: Jonathan Cape.

Prins, H. (1995) *Offenders, Deviants or Patients?* London: Routledge.

Case notes: Peter

Peter is the middle child of three siblings. When his younger sister was born his mother developed post-natal depression, and found it impossible to cope with three small children. Peter was overactive as a child and wanted constant attention. If this was not immediately given, he had temper tantrums and was aggressive and destructive, prompting his mother to 'give in' to his demands rather than risk a confrontation.

Peter's father was often away on business, but when he was at home his parents constantly argued and he often witnessed his father hitting his mother. At school, Peter was often in trouble for fighting, and was excluded at the age of seven years old for assaulting a teacher. Peter's parents were increasingly unable to cope with his behaviour by this time, and he was placed with foster parents and referred to a child psychologist. With the help of the psychologist, his foster parents established firm boundaries from the onset to which Peter responded well.

After a year Peter returned to live with his mother. His parents had separated while he had been in foster care, and he did not see his father again until he was 16. Within weeks of returning home, Peter's violent arguments with his mother began again. At the age of ten Peter began mixing with a group of 12-year-olds, staying out until late at night and smoking cigarettes and drinking alcohol, which led to his first police caution for shoplifting at the age of 11.

He reacted violently whenever his mother tried to prevent him leaving the house, and ignored her pleas for him to return home at a reasonable time. Peter's mother never reported the assaults to the police. At the age of 11 Peter began using ecstasy and amphetamines. Initially he funded this by shoplifting and stealing money from his mother's purse. In time he began to sell drugs to local school children. By this time Peter was a pupil at a special needs school, but was an infrequent attender.

At the age of 16 Peter was arrested and charged with aggravated burglary. While on bail he took a paracetamol overdose, and was seen by a psychiatrist who prescribed anti-depressants and offered him out-patient appointments, which he did not attend.

Peter received his first custodial sentence at the age of 17. Since then he has been a sentenced prisoner several times and spent long periods as a remanded prisoner, mainly because he fails to comply with the conditions of bail or community sentence orders. When in prison Peter spends a lot of time in segregation for assaults on other prisoners and officers.

Peter's relationships have mainly been of short duration. The longest lasted six months and ended when he was sent to prison for assaulting her while she was pregnant with his child. Peter has never seen his child who is now five years old. Peter has not seen his parents or sisters for a number of years, and he has few friends other than several criminal associates.

In addition to spending periods in custody Peter has also had a number of admissions to psychiatric units as a result of taking overdoses. These admissions are often of short duration because of Peter's disruptive behaviour, often fuelled by drugs or alcohol. He rarely attends out-patient appointments.

Peter's most recent conviction was for a serious assault on a nurse while under the influence of alcohol, for which Peter received a two-year custodial sentence. While serving this sentence he became severely depressed and was assessed by the prison's mental health in-reach team and admitted to a secure psychiatric unit. At the onset of this admission Peter attempted to intimidate and manipulate the nursing staff as he had done on previous admissions. However, unlike his previous admissions the multi-disciplinary team set firm boundaries on his behaviour.

Initially, Peter was only allowed to leave the ward with a nurse escort. Visitors to the ward were vetted by the multi-disciplinary team so he had no access to drugs and alcohol. He soon discovered that the staff checked everything he said with each other. Any changes to his treatment were discussed and agreed by the team. He was also encouraged to attend occupational therapy.

Initially, Peter reacted against the treatment programme. However, he soon found that he achieved more by cooperating with the team rather than trying to fight against them as he had previously done. Peter's mood began to lift. The multi-disciplinary team decided that Peter could have half an hour unescorted leave in the grounds twice a day on the condition that he agreed to random drugs screening. For the first three weeks this went well. Peter returned within the allotted time and the drug screens proved negative. During the fourth week Peter returned to the ward within the half an hour but in an excited and argumentative mood. A saliva test showed positive for amphetamines and his leave was stopped immediately. On being told this, Peter threw a chair across the room. The police were called and he was charged with criminal damage.

When the effects of the amphetamines had worn off, Peter told the multi-disciplinary team that while out in the grounds he decided that 'a line of whizz' would lift his mood so called a friend. Following several more occasions such as this, Peter claimed that 'something had changed'. He was now 28 and had spent most of his adult life in either hospital or prison. He had re-established contact with his mother and sisters, and had even been able to talk to them about the effect his behaviour had had on them in previous years. After a further six months in hospital the multi-disciplinary team began discussing discharge with Peter, with referral to a therapeutic community being the preferred option for both him and the staff.

Peter (continued)

Peter was accepted at a therapeutic community but found it difficult fitting in with the group, especially once he discovered that he was the only member of the community that had not been sexually abused. He found it difficult sitting in groups listening to other group members talking of their experiences, and believed he had nothing in common with the other residents. After three weeks he walked out.

Peter returned to his home town and soon returned to his old ways. Within a month he was arrested for burglary and possession with intent to supply. He received a custodial sentence, became severely depressed and was referred to the psychiatrist under whose care he had been during his last hospital admission. This time he was treated in prison by the prison's mental health in-reach team. Prior to his release a care programme approach (CPA) meeting was held and a care coordinator was allocated to him. On release from prison Peter went to live in a supported hostel for ex-offenders. The hostel imposed firm boundaries and Peter was asked to sign an abstinence agreement as a condition of tenancy. He agreed to his care coordinator carrying out regular drug screens and attended regular appointments with the psychiatrist.

Peter has been at the hostel for 18 months now. He has a small circle of friends, and works as a labourer for a local builder, which at the age of 31 is his first ever paid employment. He is also attending an evening computer course at college. He is in regular contact with his family and has recently met his daughter for the first time. The next challenge for Peter will be moving into independent accommodation.

Peter: points for reflection

1. Which factors in Peter's early life might have caused difficulties for him in adulthood?

2. Like many people with a personality disorder, Peter is not formally 'diagnosed' as such. Is there sufficient evidence for a personality disorder to be identified, and if so, what difference might this make to his support and treatment?

3. What are Peter's needs?

4. Which aspects of Peter's care (both in hospital and in the supported housing) have most benefited him in the long term?

Handout 5.1 What's in a name?

The recognized disease classification systems break mental disorder down into a bewildering array of categories and sub-types. The current *International Classification of Diseases (ICD-10)* (World Health Organization 1992) suggests nine separate types of personality disorder, although its 'F60.8 Other specific personality disorders' category includes a further six sub-categories! On the other hand, the *DSM-IV* (American Psychiatric Association 2000) lists ten separate categories. The component parts of these classification systems are rarely used in practice as the personality traits and behaviours of each category invariably overlap with one another. However, *DSM-IV* provides a solution to this problem by grouping the sub-categories of personality disorder into three broad 'clusters' that are more widely used in both day-to-day practice and research. Some (but not all) of the more frequently observed types of personality disorder are outlined here. Seeing the different types in this context may go some way to explaining why only *some* categories come to the attention of mental health services, while others may have a significant impact on a person's life without necessarily attracting the attention of mental health or other support services.

Cluster A: the 'odd' or 'eccentric' types

Cluster A includes the paranoid, schizoid and schizotypal personality disorders. People with cluster A disorders are suspicious or even paranoid toward others, and have great difficulty forming relationships with other people, or may even avoid human contact altogether. Their daily routine and lifestyle is aimed at avoidance of social situations or particular people, and tend not to come to local attention or are simply described by neighbours as 'odd', 'eccentric' or 'weird'.

Although it is relatively unusual for cluster A personality disorder to be seen in psychiatric clinics or in-patient units, clinicians are careful to make a distinction between personality disorder on the one hand, and a psychotic illness such as schizophrenia on the other. While terms such as 'paranoid' and 'schizoid' suggest a close similarity with severe mental illnesses such as schizophrenia, cluster A disorders are not *psychotic* disorders. Distrust and suspicion in this context are personality traits as opposed to symptoms of mental illness and will not usually respond to treatment with anti-psychotic drugs. This is a particularly important distinction where issues of drug treatment or detention under the Mental Health Act are under consideration.

Cluster B: the 'dramatic', 'emotional' or 'erratic' types

This cluster includes the histrionic, narcissistic, anti-social and borderline personality disorders, and is perhaps the most familiar to those working in mental health. Borderline and anti-social personality disorder will be particularly familiar to care staff, and warrant more detailed individual discussion.

Borderline personality disorder (BPD) refers to the symptoms being on the borderline between psychosis and neurosis. BPD is characterized by impulsivity, unstable personal relationships and poor self-esteem. People with BPD are often highly ambivalent in their feelings toward others, veering from positive to negative opinions about others while being fearful of abandonment, which they will go to considerable lengths to avoid. Another frequently described feeling is a sensation of 'emptiness' and lack of emotions of any kind.

People with BPD are also highly susceptible to stress, and may react strongly and sometimes dramatically to situations that would not trouble most people. They are prone to self-harm, or sometimes threaten to commit suicide, particularly when they feel rejected or believe that relationships (whether personal or professional) are about to end. As with other forms of personality disorder, BPD is often associated with other mental disorders such as depression or psychosis, and under particular duress the person may become abnormally suspicious or paranoid. BPD is often seen as an essentially 'female' disorder, but while the majority of clients coming to the attention of care professionals will be female this is certainly not a condition exclusive to women.

On the other hand, anti-social personality disorder (ASPD) tends to be more prevalent among men than women, and is particularly common among both remand and sentenced male prisoners. People with ASPD have a typically anti-authoritarian attitude, do not conform to social norms or laws, and have a tendency toward repeated aggressive and upsetting behaviour, with little or no remorse shown or consideration for how their behaviour has affected those around them. They have a flagrant disregard for feelings, and often lie or manipulate situations for personal gain, even when it is obvious that their actions will harm or upset other people. Like other personality disorders, ASPD is an adult condition, although diagnosis will also depend on disruptive and aggressive behaviour in childhood and adolescence, with school exclusion a very common feature of the person's history.

Cluster C: the 'anxious' and 'fearful' types

Cluster C includes obsessive-compulsive, dependent and avoidant personality disorders. These are possibly the least likely of the personality disorders to be seen in mental health or community services, and will often apply to people living otherwise normal lives, albeit with particular and often quite difficult problems in terms of work, relationships and lifestyle.

✓

In many ways, obsessive-compulsive personality disorder is almost a diametrical opposite of dependent personality disorder. The former type might often be seen in those commonly described as 'control freaks', 'workaholics' and 'perfectionists'. In common with other types, obsessive-compulsive personality disorder is characterized by an inability to show tenderness or warmth to others or to trust anyone else but themselves with even the simplest of tasks. Individuals become obsessed with work or, in some cases, hobbies and interests, often to the exclusion of all else. They are unhappy with anything less than complete perfection in a given task or piece of work, which must be 'just right' with nothing left to chance.

On the other hand, people with dependent personality disorder are excessively passive, handing responsibility for every area of life to other people. They have little self-confidence and are often completely unable to function independently, often depending almost entirely on the care of a relative or partner for even the simplest of tasks. It is not uncommon for someone with this disorder to have no conception of, for example, a bank account or how to pay household bills. They will often remain non-drivers throughout their lives and may remain unemployed for many years.

Handout 5.2 Treating personality disorder

Personality disordered individuals present enormous difficulties and challenges to mental health workers, and invariably spark debate as to the validity of categorizing personality as 'normal' or 'abnormal'. Furthermore, mental health professionals often disagree on the 'treatability' of personality disorder, although it is widely acknowledged that in-patient units seldom provide anything other than short-term respite or crisis intervention for patients. These arguments have contributed to something of a 'postcode lottery' in terms of the treatment and resources available to this client group. In fact, the extent to which personality disordered people can access appropriate services depends largely on the extent to which local resources both acknowledge personality disorder, and believe that such individuals can be successfully helped (National Institute for Mental Health in England 2003). This state of affairs has prompted recent high-level initiatives to encourage local providers to develop specialized services for this client group, with increased funding for resources and care packages based on an increasingly solid evidence base for effective treatment and support.

While it is certainly the case that the resources outlined here are specialist, scarce and demand intensive extra training, approaches such as these are coming under increasing scrutiny and research, and in the absence of an effective and specific drug treatment for personality disorder, the 'talking treatments' along with the often invaluable contribution of the housing and community care agencies represent an increasingly optimistic outlook on what used to be described as the 'diagnosis of exclusion'.

We shall outline some of the more well-established approaches, and while they differ in theoretical basis and method, some common underlying principles have been described that appear to be constant in the more promising approaches. They tend to be well structured, have a clear focus, emphasize the importance of compliance with the therapy, and must actually 'make sense' to the patient. Furthermore, the treatments that garner the most optimism tend to emphasize the attachment between therapist and patient, are relatively long term in nature, and are well integrated with other services with which the recipient might be involved.

The therapeutic community approach

Therapeutic communities are perhaps the oldest and most well established of treatments for personality disorder, although it could be argued that they represent an 'approach' rather than a psychiatric treatment in the usual sense. The story of their development is surprising. Faced with the prospect of treating huge numbers of combat-traumatized soldiers during World War II, military psychiatrists Tom Main and Maxwell Jones established communities at military hospitals in Birmingham and North London respectively, where the boundaries of traditional doctor–nurse–patient roles became increasingly unimportant against a backdrop of shared experiences and group discussion.

Both Main and Jones continued their work long after the war had ended, and founded the Cassel and Henderson Hospitals respectively, both of which continue to this day as important centres of excellence in the treatment of personality disorder. Therapeutic communities are, in essence, small, cohesive communities whose members are made up of both staff and patients, and where all members participate in decision-making, rule formation and the day-to-day running of the community. Group therapy and discussion underpin the day-to-day activities against an ethos of communalism and respect for the behaviour and feelings of others, although anti-social or disruptive actions are discussed and, if necessary, sanctioned by the community. Although the community consists of both 'patients' and paid professional staff, the more traditional inter-discipline hierarchy and boundaries between staff and patients are 'flattened'.

While this approach has helped many thousands of personality disordered individuals, and studies have suggested optimism in treating those who (in many cases) have been deemed 'untreatable' (Dolan, Warren and Norton 1997; Lees, Manning and Rawlings 1999), there remain barriers to their wider establishment and development. First, those most likely to benefit from this approach are in many ways least likely to commit to such a long-term and intensive process, even when they have been referred to a service and accepted by the community itself. Second, therapeutic communities demand a high level of commitment on the part of professional staff, who must be prepared to work in ways that vary widely from the more traditional models of psychiatric care to which they may be accustomed. Nonetheless, the therapeutic community approach has now been applied to an increasingly wide variety of settings such as day care centres and even the prison system, and while the success of treatment is yet to be unequivocally proved by rigorous research (Rutter and Tyrer 2003) there remains both optimism and anecdotal evidence for the efficacy of this approach.

The cognitive approach

The cognitive approach to therapy with personality disordered people encompasses several different types of talking treatment that are currently being researched and validated in terms of their usefulness for this client group. The best known of these is cognitive behaviour therapy (CBT) (see Chapter 2 Treatment and Support) but other variations on the cognitive theme, where patients are helped to examine and modify their own thoughts and feelings by a trained therapist, have emerged in recent years as potentially useful means of addressing personality disorder.

Dialectical behaviour therapy (DBT)

DBT was initially developed to treat women with borderline personality disorder, with a specific remit to reduce incidents of self-harm and stabilize chaotic lifestyles. Recent initiatives are now underway to widen its remit to male patients and to address other forms of personality disorder.

DBT is usually a group-oriented therapy, and in many ways is reminiscent of a training course. One of the key aspects of personality disorder is the fact that many of those identified as having this condition are never aware, or never accept that they have been diagnosed or labelled in this way. One of the aims of DBT is to educate group members about their disorder, as well as looking at their own feelings and behaviours in detail and learning new coping skills to cope with stress, and replace familiar responses such as self-harm, substance abuse or aggression.

Based on a core principle of positive relationships between clients and their specially trained therapists, DBT has yet to be thoroughly and independently researched, although initial results and anecdotal evidence have suggested some possibilities, particularly in the reduction of critical incidents such as self-harm (Bateman and Tyrer 2002).

Cognitive analytical therapy (CAT)

Recent years have seen a growing interest in the use of this therapy in addressing the problems associated with borderline personality disorder. When applied in this context, CAT is based on the theory that BPD represents a set of 'self-states'. In other words, the person experiences a number of distinct moods and behaviours and rapidly swings between these states according to external influences such as stress, relationships or tasks. The person has little or no ability to control their emotions as they switch from one 'self-state' to another, and therapy is essentially a working collaboration between therapist and patient in which the latter's self-states are identified in both day-to-day life and within the therapy sessions themselves.

CAT integrates cognitive and psychoanalytic ideas, although the emphasis is firmly on description and the 'here and now' as opposed to the interpretation and reflection more readily associated with psychoanalysis. CAT is structured and time-limited, with pen and paper exercises and homework representing much of the therapeutic body of the treatment. There is as yet little empirical evidence for the efficacy of this approach, although a number of studies are in progress to evaluate the use of CAT with personality disordered individuals in a variety of settings.

✓

Pharmacological treatments

Given the lack of resources and difficulties in applying some or all of the type of talking treatments outlined above, and the occasional necessity of admitting personality disordered patients to psychiatric units in times of crisis, it is unsurprising that drug treatments (such as anti-depressants, anti-psychotics and mood stabilizers) are a frequently used resource despite the lack of a specific treatment for this condition and the general reluctance to further 'medicalize' personality disorder or induce dependence on the part of patients. However, personality disorder is often associated with 'comorbid' conditions such as depression or anxiety, which can be successfully treated with medication. Limited and careful prescription of SSRI anti-depressants and anxiolytics has been seen to have some part to play in the treatment of specific problem behaviours and the resolution of short-term distress or crisis which may require considerable 'damping' before the individual can begin to work in a more psychological way or respond to professionals using the interpersonal skills outlined elsewhere in this chapter.

Handout 5.3 Personality disorder and the Mental Health Act

The current Mental Health Act (MHA) uses the term 'psychopathy' to describe that spectrum of personality traits and behaviours that warrant compulsory medical intervention and detention. The term 'psychopath' has, of course, been a staple of films and tabloid headlines for many years, but the MHA uses the title as a point of reference for those who have a persistent tendency to engage in 'seriously irresponsible conduct' and whose condition is deemed by clinicians to be amenable to treatment. For those responsible for decisions regarding the detention and treatment of the personality disordered (or psychopath in this legal context), the definition of 'seriously irresponsible conduct' is highly problematic. It could be argued, for example, that this description could represent much of the current prison population, the many thousands of people who deliberately harm themselves, and even those who indulge in dangerous sports such as hang-gliding or extreme rock climbing.

This question perhaps underpins the well-known variation in the way that personality disorder is approached by mental health professionals at both a team and individual level. The 'treatability' of personality disorder is perhaps one of the most contested issues in mental health care, and is debated regularly at both a clinical and management level. Recent developments in the UK have placed personality disorder towards the top of the mental health agenda, with plans being made to establish centres where high-risk individuals with a diagnosis of personality disorder can be treated in secure conditions by specialist staff (Department of Health/Home Office 1999).

The determination of 'treatability' is equally (if not more) difficult and the cause of much debate between clinicians. Drug treatments which are known to be effective in treating mental illness and can be forcibly administered if necessary, are not effective in treating personality disorder. Psychological therapies such as CBT or counselling, while undoubtedly having some place in the treatment of this condition, depend on a partnership between patient and therapist, are long term in nature and certainly cannot be administered against a person's will.

Given these arguments it is unsurprising that 'psychopathic disorder' accounts for only a tiny minority (about 5%) of all compulsory admissions to hospital compared with the 'mental illness' category (88%). In fact, almost two-thirds of compulsory admissions under the psychopathy category are imposed via the courts following criminal convictions (Office for National Statistics 2005).

✓

Even the most experienced mental health professionals have great difficulty agreeing with each other on the diagnosis of personality disorder, although both *DSM-IV* and *ICD-10* offer reasonably straightforward definitions. For example, *DSM-IV* defines personality disorder as:

> an enduring pattern of inner experience and behaviour that deviates markedly from the expectations of the individual's culture, is pervasive and inflexible, has an onset in adolescence or early adulthood, is stable over time, and leads to distress or impairment. (American Psychiatric Association 2000, p.685–731)

The standardized criteria by which doctors diagnose illnesses are useful when trying to identify appendicitis, but applying a medical label to the vagaries of human behaviour is an altogether more complex process. Unlike mental illnesses, which are recognized and treated in much the same way throughout the developed world, the diagnosis of personality disorder depends to a large part on a deviation from social and cultural norms which change from one population to the next. What might be seen as anti-social and destructive behaviour by a rural community may merit little more than a shrug of the shoulders in a deprived inner-city estate. An otherwise 'normal' social interaction on the streets of London may be seen as grossly offensive in Japan.

Furthermore, the recognized criteria for personality disorder would apply to most of us at various times and within different contexts, although diagnosis depends on personality traits and behaviours being reported *consistently* over a period of time and causing the individual (and those around them) significant problems in their day-to-day lives.

Both classification systems sub-divide personality disorder into a number of categories such as 'histrionic', 'anti-social' or 'narcissistic', but these are largely regarded as unwieldy and difficult to validate as few clinicians are able to agree a 'clean' differentiation between one category and another due to the widely overlapping nature of the personality traits accredited to each diagnostic label. *DSM-IV* does offer a relatively useful 'cluster' system (see Handout 5.1 What's in a name?), which represents a reasonably accessible means of understanding how clinicians diagnose and study personality disorder and how the condition actually manifests to both the sufferer and those around them. But how do these textbook definitions of personality disorder actually relate to those individuals seen by mental health workers in day-to-day practice, and why is this such an unpopular and controversial diagnosis?

A large proportion of those who meet the diagnostic criteria will never be aware that they have a personality disorder and will never come into contact with a mental health professional, although they may come into contact with the police or draw attention to themselves within their local community. However, they will certainly be more likely than most to have what mental health professionals call a 'comorbid' mental disorder such as substance dependence or a psychotic illness (Weaver *et al.* 2002), and those that engage in persistently self-destructive or anti-social behaviours (the so-called 'cluster B' individuals) are more likely to come to the attention of mental health services, supported housing and other care agencies.

Personality disorder characteristics

- a range of abnormal personality 'traits' that characterize how an individual acts and feels

- medical condition or social problem?

- incidence of one in ten: higher in offender and substance misuse populations

- failed relationships, difficulty forming bonds with others, potential to create distress for individual and others

- 'black and white thinking', anti-authoritarian attitudes, irresponsible, unreliable

- gradual onset from childhood; for example, ADHD, school exclusion

- usually preceded by unhappy family background, but genetic factors may also be important.

Personality disorder diagnosis

A diagnosis of exclusion?

- poor outcomes from normal in-patient treatment

- wide variation in attitudes to treatment of clinicians and services

- some success demonstrated with therapeutic techniques; for example, therapeutic community approach, dialectical behaviour therapy (DBT).

The 'cluster' system

- *DSM-IV* definition: 'an enduring pattern of inner experience and behaviour that deviates markedly from the expectations of the individual's culture, is pervasive and inflexible, has an onset in adolescence or early adulthood, is stable over time, and leads to distress or impairment'

- three diagnostic clusters:

    1. cluster A: the 'odd' or 'eccentric' types

    2. cluster B: the 'dramatic', 'emotional' or 'erratic' types

    3. cluster C: the 'anxious' and 'fearful' types.

Chapter 6

Working with People who Self-harm

Many thousands of people cut, burn or poison themselves on a regular basis. For most people this is a behaviour that is difficult, if not impossible, to understand. Self-harm is remarkably common and, for those who practise it regularly, is a compulsive act without which life becomes unbearable.

The prevalence of self-harm is difficult to assess. There are approximately 150,000 accident and emergency episodes each year as a result of self-harm (Kapur *et al.* 1998), but general and psychiatric hospital figures will only represent that proportion of people who have attended for treatment, and do not include the many for whom self-harm is a secretive activity seldom requiring emergency treatment or psychiatric intervention.

A recent interview survey in the UK (Meltzer *et al.* 2002) suggested that 2 per cent of men and 3 per cent of women have deliberately harmed themselves at some point in their lives without the intention to kill themselves. The same survey revealed that the prevalence decreases rapidly with age, and is more prevalent among single (including separated and divorced) unemployed women, with self-harm appearing to be significantly associated with mental disorder and drug and alcohol dependence.

Self-harm appears to becoming increasingly common among adolescents. A survey of school-age children (Hawton *et al.* 2002) revealed that 13 per cent of young people aged 15 or 16 reported having self-harmed at some time in their lives, with 7 per cent having done so within the previous year. The same study revealed that adolescent girls may be three times more likely to self-harm than boys.

What is self-harm?

Self-harm is the deliberate injury to body tissue without the intention to kill oneself. It is a means of inflicting pain, discomfort and injury to one's own body by a wide variety of means including cutting, burning, scalding, hitting, or ingesting/inserting poisons or foreign bodies. Even experienced housing and mental health workers never fail to be surprised by the varied and sometimes bizarre methods used by people who are intent on harming themselves.

Self-harm is not in itself a mental disorder, but a manifestation of distress that may or may not be associated with mental health problems. Many people who deliberately injure themselves do so as part of an otherwise normal lifestyle, in much the same way as other forms of self-injury such as smoking, drinking, taking drugs or even body piercing. The double Olympic gold medal winner Kelly Holmes is a recent example of someone who has practised self-harm as part of an otherwise normal (and highly successful) life (Holmes 2005). Nonetheless, the more frequent and often severe forms of self-harm are behaviours often encountered by mental health workers at all levels.

Self-harm is difficult to comprehend for most care workers, but for those who have practised it (sometimes for many years) these are deeply ingrained behaviours that cannot be changed 'overnight', even assuming that the client actually wants to change at all.

Suicide and self-harm

Self-harm and suicide are often thought of as one and the same, but are very different phenomena. Self-harm is not an attempt to commit suicide but is conversely described as a means of survival. The differences between suicide and self-harm cause much confusion, and while a careful assessment of suicide risk is an essential aspect of care for this client group (see Handout 6.2 Key risk factors for suicide and Chapter 3 Risk Assessment and Management) this section will aim to make these differences a little clearer and dispel some common myths.

There are nearly 6000 deaths by suicide per year in the UK (Office for National Statistics 2005), although the true figure is likely to be much higher. This is because a death is recorded by a coroner as suicide only when there is very strong evidence (for example, a letter or note) to support the assumption that a person has taken their own life. Some sudden deaths are officially recorded as 'accidental death' or 'misadventure' when in fact the deceased has intended to end their own life. For coroners, the standard of proof for suicide is set very high.

Another common misconception is that suicide is almost always associated with depression or some other psychiatric disorder. In fact, a recent UK study has shown that only one-quarter of those recorded as having killed themselves have had any recent contact with mental health professionals or GPs prior to death (Appleby et al. 2001). This is not to say that the other 75 per cent were not suffering from psychological distress, but this figure would certainly suggest that many people commit suicide as a response to unhappy relationships, business failures, poor physical health, terminal illness or any other significant life event.

Reliable statistics for the incidence of self-harm are difficult to come by as researchers are faced with significant problems of description and definition.

Injuries are often 'one off' events rather than frequent behaviours, and as mentioned earlier, many individuals cut or burn themselves as part and parcel of an otherwise normal life, only infrequently requiring medical help for self-sustained injuries that have perhaps been more severe than usual.

Most general hospitals now have liaison psychiatry staff on duty, whose role often involves the assessment of patients admitted with self-inflicted injuries, only a small proportion of whom will require further psychiatric intervention. Of this group, the self-harm will usually be frequent or particularly severe, or the person may be assessed as having mental health problems requiring further assessment and/or treatment.

To challenge another myth, it is often thought that those wishing to commit suicide simply 'get on with it' in silence while self-harm is often loudly announced in threats and warnings, mainly as a means of 'attention seeking'. The need to draw attention to oneself can sometimes be a factor, but is certainly not an exclusive motivating factor. Self-harm is often a silent and highly secretive behaviour hidden from friends and family by closed doors and long-sleeved jumpers. Contrary to popular belief, suicide is often carefully planned and even signalled beforehand, although the signals, which can range from changes in financial arrangements to clear verbal warnings, are often less than obvious.

Why do people harm themselves?

Self-harm has a number of antecedents, some of which will overlap with one another. The compulsion or desire to injure oneself is extraordinarily difficult to understand, and an immediate question might be, 'Why did you do it?' Questions such as these might be well intentioned but are unlikely to elicit much in the way of a meaningful answer. 'Don't know' or 'I felt wound up' are much more likely responses. Working with clients who self-harm often means working with someone who is angry, distressed and has enormous difficulty trusting others. However, with skilled, empathic and above all, non-judgemental responses, the professional relationship has the potential to develop such that the client is able to trust workers, and may even become able to articulate their distress and identify some of the underlying issues that have driven the individual to self-harm. Some of these issues will be outlined in this section, although it is important to remember that this is not an exhaustive list, and the issues discussed here are far from mutually exclusive but will usually overlap with one another to some degree.

Taking control

It is well known that a significant proportion of people who self-harm have been subject to physical or sexual abuse during childhood (Santa-Mina and Gallop

1998). Perpetrators of abuse exert enormous power and control over the victim, often by means of threats, rewards or emotional manipulation. For a young person faced with this situation, cutting or burning is often cited as a means of exerting at least some control over what happens to their bodies, and often becomes a comforting and reliable means of dealing with problems long into adulthood.

Releasing tension

Anger and frustration are basic human drives requiring expression of one form or another. Most people are able to vent their frustrations in relatively 'appropriate' ways, although partners, pets, family members or household objects may sometimes become the unwitting targets of someone's anger. People who self-harm see their behaviour as a 'safe' way of venting frustration without hurting anyone else. They will talk of their injuries feeling akin to the 'blowing' of a valve after a period of stress and tension, often describing the sensation of pain or the sight of bleeding offering almost immediate relief from pent-up feelings (Arnold and Magill 1996).

Communication

Most people give little thought to their ability to communicate. Talking, gesturing, writing, painting or even singing are all forms of expression taken for granted. Where the ability to communicate is impaired, self-harm may be the only means by which an individual can communicate how they feel. Impaired communication may be within the context of either physical or intellectual disability, or may be environmental; for example, a restrictive family environment or institutional regime such as prison.

Care workers sometimes describe self-harm as 'attention seeking'. Terminologies such as these are usually considered misinformed and derogatory by those who self-harm, and suggest that it may be more helpful to describe such incidents as a person's attempt to communicate their distress (Fox and Hawton 2004).

Negative body image

The most common forms of self-harm such as cutting and burning leave very visible scar tissue. This is often more than incidental. As has already been seen, childhood trauma is often associated with self-harm in adulthood. A history of abusive relationships can often lead to a very poor sense of self-worth, leaving the victim feeling ugly and deserving little in the way of respect from self or others. This appears to be particularly evident when the individual has consistently failed to meet the demands of significant others, or where there is a history of sexual or physical abuse. The scars of countless burns, cuts and insertions are a very visible manifestation of this self-image, and are often described as representing the 'punishment' that the individual feels they deserve.

Stimulation

People who regularly self-harm often describe the 'buzz' they get from inflicting pain on themselves. This may be a purely sensory phenomenon, with clients likening the smell of burning flesh or the sight of blood to the elation induced by sex or drugs. In fact, this latter comparison is not so surprising. Pain causes the body to release endorphins, which are the human body's natural version of painkillers or analgesics. Endorphins can have an effect not dissimilar to opiate drugs such as morphine, and it is not uncommon for drug-using self-harmers to compare the 'rush' of drugs such as heroin or amphetamines with that of cutting one's arm or burning an arm with a cigarette.

Mental disorder

Given that self-harm is such a seemingly bizarre behaviour, the casual observer might be forgiven for assuming that this is a 'psychiatric' phenomenon requiring intervention from mental health services. Self-harm is not a mental disorder in itself, although persistent and severe injuries can indicate an underlying problem requiring further assessment and, if necessary, treatment. Self-harm is one of the key diagnostic features of borderline personality disorder (see Chapter 5 Working with Personality Disorder), and can also feature in conditions such as schizophrenia and depression, sometimes in response to hallucinations or delusions.

In residential or community placements where clients are younger and have little in the way of recorded histories, it is essential to seek a detailed professional assessment as soon as possible, particularly where, for example, prolonged social withdrawal, odd behaviours, disjointed speech or sleep and mood disturbance are observed.

Helping people who self-harm

A recent review of treatment approaches to self-harm (National Collaborating Centre for Mental Health 2004) failed to identify any specific medical or psychological approach that stands out as an effective response to self-harming behaviour, although there is limited evidence for the efficacy of dialectical behaviour therapy (DBT) (see Chapter 5 Working with Personality Disorder) where self-harm is part of a borderline personality disorder. However, there is strong anecdotal evidence from the NCCMH report that for those who deliberately injure themselves, professional responses are often negative and lacking in empathy. There are several potential reasons behind such antipathy (see Handout 6.1 An attitude problem?) but perceived helplessness on the part of mental health workers is undoubtedly one of the factors. This section will outline some of the most useful techniques for both helping people who self-harm, and facilitating more positive and optimistic attitudes among those who work with them.

Of course, prior to offering support to someone who deliberately injures themselves, two key points of clarification are required:

- Does self-harm actually present a problem for that person?

- Are they clear that they wish to work on changing their behaviour or trying to identify underlying factors? (See Handout 6.3 Some points of caution.)

The self-harm toolkit

The now familiar toolkit is a set of roles that care staff can use to better understand both self-harm itself, and the clients who practise it.

The pragmatist

While occasionally occurring as a 'one off' incident, self-harm is usually a regular and frequent practice that is part of a person's life, in some cases since childhood. The pragmatist is able to accept that self-harm, as difficult as it is to understand, is often an important and essential part of an individual's survival and well-being. It will not cease 'overnight' and will sometimes be a part of that person's life indefinitely. Nonetheless, the pragmatist is able to point out that this is potentially dangerous behaviour and seeks to help the person understand why they feel the need to hurt themselves. The pragmatist offers support in trying to replace cutting, burning or overdosing with safer ways of expressing their distress or communicating with others.

The pragmatist might suggest negotiating a 'self-harm contract' with a client, whereby their injuries are limited to a fixed time, place and method, perhaps with a gradual reduction in frequency and/or severity and the offer of one-to-one support when the person is feeling particularly vulnerable and likely to self-harm.

If cutting is the primary form of injury, the pragmatic worker might also suggest that a first aid kit be kept by the client, and demonstrate how they might dress their own wounds safely and hygienically, with further advice as to immediate actions should injuries be more severe than usual. Such techniques are, of course, at the discretion and direction of an organization's policies and procedures, and should be agreed and carried out with the full knowledge of colleagues and managers.

The tranquillizer

The self-harming client may be able to endure significant degrees of pain and in many cases may actually seek gratification from the sight of flowing blood or burnt skin. This is not to say that they will not be afraid, ashamed or angry before, during or after an incident. The tranquillizer is able to remain calm in the face of both considerable distress and sometimes disturbing scenes.

MEDICATION?

In some cases, pharmacological means of reducing arousal and distress may be necessary. While medication is certainly not a long-term solution to what is an extremely complex set of problems and behaviours, people who self-harm can often become completely overwhelmed by distress or anger to the extent that support or psychological interventions are of limited use. Where clients are severely distressed, the careful prescription of sedative medication may be of some value, at least in the short term. It is worth noting that many of the more commonly prescribed tranquillizers and hypnotics (sleeping tablets) are dependence-inducing and will have only a short-term therapeutic benefit. While self-harm is not a mental disorder in itself, it is a behaviour that often forms part of a broader mental disorder such as depression, which can be treated with appropriate medication as part of a wider care plan of support and practical help.

The inventor

The inventor is a role that may become as ultimately important for clients to take on as for those who support them. The inventor helps suggest ways and means of deflecting the urge to self-harm. Alternatives can be sought in quite simple distractions such as listening to music, going for a walk or punching a pillow. The act of self-harm is often impulsive, and can sometimes be 'bypassed' long enough for the urge to dissipate. Similarly, clients can be helped to look at ways that they might place obstacles in the way of self-injury, particularly where an individual's self-harm is of a more impulsive nature. If the client has a favourite 'weapon' such as a piece of glass, razor blade or cigarette lighter, access to this item can be negotiated with the person and made at least temporarily inaccessible, delaying self-harm long enough for the initial impulse to subside.

Clients might also be encouraged to try alternative ways of communicating their feelings. This may be in the usual verbal sense, although other mediums such as writing, drawing or music can also be helpful, particularly where the person has difficulty articulating how they feel.

References

Appleby, L., Shaw, J., Sherrat, J., Amos, T., Robinson, J., McDonnell, R., *et al.* (2001) *Safety First: Report of the National Confidential Inquiry into Suicide and Homicide by People with Mental Illness.* London: Stationery Office.

Arnold, L. and Magill, A. (1996) *Working with Self-injury: A Practical Guide.* Abergavenny: The Basement Project.

Fox, C. and Hawton, K. (2004) *Deliberate Self-harm in Adolescence.* London: Jessica Kingsley Publishers.

Hawton, K., Rodham, K., Evans, E. and Weatherall, R. (2002) 'Deliberate self-harm in adolescents: self-report survey in schools in England.' *British Medical Journal 325*, 7374, 1207–1211.

Holmes, K. (2005) *Black, White and Gold – The Autobiography.* London: Virgin Books.

Kapur, N., House, A., Creed, F., Feldman, E., Friedman, T. and Guthrie, E. (1998) 'Management of deliberate self-poisoning in adults in four teaching hospitals: descriptive study.' *British Medical Journal 316*, 7134, 831–832.

Meltzer, H., Jenkins, K., Singleton, S., Charlton, J. and Yar, M. (2002) *Non-fatal Suicidal Behaviour Among Adults Aged 16 to 74 in Great Britain.* London: Stationery Office.

National Collaborating Centre for Mental Health (2004) *Self-harm: The Short-term Physical and Psychological Management and Secondary Prevention of Self-harm in Primary and Secondary Care.* Leicester: The British Psychological Society.

Office for National Statistics (2005) *Suicide Rates in England and Wales, 2000 to 2003.* London: Stationery Office.

Santa-Mina, E. and Gallop, R. (1998) 'Childhood sexual and physical abuse and adult self-harm and suicidal behaviour: a literature review.' *Canadian Journal of Psychiatry 43*, 8, 793–800.

Useful resources

Websites

Bristol Crisis Service for Women: www.users.zetnet.co.uk/bcsw

National Children's Bureau/Young People and Self Harm: www.selfharm.org.uk

The National Self Harm Network: www.nshn.co.uk

Books

Alderman, T. (1997) *The Scarred Soul: Understanding and Ending Self-inflicted Violence.* Oakland, CA: New Harbinger Publications.

Arnold, L. (1998) *Self-help for Self-injury: A Guide to Women Struggling with Self-injury.* Bristol: Bristol Crisis Service For Women.

Bird, L. and Faulkner, A. (2000) *Suicide and Self Harm.* London: The Mental Health Foundation.

National Self Harm Network (1999) *Cutting the Risk: Self Harm, Self Care and Risk Reduction.* Rochdale: National Self Harm Network.

✓

Case notes: Donna

Donna began harming herself when she was ten, and ran away from home at 15. She has not spoken to her family since. She has slept rough or stayed with friends and acquaintances in various towns and cities around the country. Now 20 years old Donna has eked out a living by begging or, occasionally, prostitution.

Donna cuts her arms with anything sharp, although she favours a clean razor blade and makes superficial wounds on her upper arms and torso. Her self-harming increases at times of stress, and she becomes angry and even aggressive if she is unable to cut herself when her urges compel her to do so. Occasionally Donna has made particularly deep cuts and has been admitted to hospital for sutures. She has been assessed by mental health professionals in accident and emergency departments but has always been resistive and evasive when assessed, and has vehemently refuted any suggestion that she has any form of mental health problem.

Finding herself homeless once again, Donna has been staying at a direct access shelter for two weeks. She has told her keyworker that she does not care what happens to her and says that she sometimes wishes she does not wake up. She described herself as being in 'constant pain', and that hurting herself is the only way to numb this pain. If she does not cut herself regularly, she becomes tense, anxious and irritable.

After several incidents of quite severe lacerations to her arms and legs, her keyworker has suggested that Donna hand in her razor blades and comes to speak with a member of staff whenever she feels the urge to cut herself. She replies that she does not feel confident about talking to anyone other than her keyworker, but she will consider handing in her 'sharps'. She eventually reveals to her keyworker that she was sexually abused by her father and other male relatives for as long as she could remember, forcing her to run away from home while still a teenager. She continues to feel like 'a dirty slag' and sees disfigurement and continued sexual abuse in the world of prostitution as fitting punishment for her childhood behaviour.

After a few days, Donna has decided to give her razor blades and a knife that she had hidden to staff, but has still resorted to burning her arms with cigarettes on several occasions. Meanwhile, Donna's keyworker has arranged for her to move on to a longer-term placement, and is working with her to use distraction techniques such as listening to a personal stereo (at very loud volume) whenever she feels the need to injure herself. Although she is upset that she will lose contact with her keyworker when she moves on, she acknowledges that her time at the direct access shelter has been invaluable in acknowledging some of her feelings about her past, and in recognizing that there are at least some people whom she can trust.

Donna: points for reflection

1. Is Donna at risk of killing herself?

2. If Donna were able to articulate why she harms herself, what reasons might she describe?

3. Do you think that Donna suffers from a mental health problem?

4. What is most important in Donna's keyworker's ability to form a trusting relationship with her?

5. Is total 'abstinence' from self-harm an appropriate goal for Donna?

Handout 6.1 An attitude problem?

Anecdotal evidence suggests that a more empathic and positive response to self-harm is becoming more prevalent among health and social care workers. Nonetheless, cutting, overdoses and cigarette burns continue to evoke a variety of negative and unhelpful attitudes from many workers (National Collaborating Centre for Mental Health 2004). Faced with the often constant demands of assessing wounds, ensuring treatment via a GP or accident and emergency department, and filling in the inevitable incident forms and completing client records, it is perhaps unsurprising how workers are faced with a sense of helplessness and frustration, particularly where staff resources are limited and a client's behaviour is purposeful and cannot be attributed to the symptoms of severe mental illness. This 'bad not mad' attitude is a frequent attribution made by care staff. A person with schizophrenia might cut their wrists in response to auditory hallucinations or delusional beliefs, but when the same act is carried out by someone who is otherwise 'well' (particularly as a regular occurrence) this is often seen as a planned, wilful act, which is, therefore, incomprehensible and frustrating.

Self-harm has the potential to make workers feel angry, frustrated, upset, or even nauseous, and provokes a variety of explanations and analyses that often fail to help clients address underlying causes. For example, workers may use terms such as 'attention seeking' to describe a client's self-inflicted injury. For many self-harming clients, their attempts to communicate needs or seek affection will have been met from a very early age by punishment, abuse or dismissal. Within an institutional setting such as a psychiatric unit or shared housing, self-harm may well be a means of seeking attention from staff, but is perhaps that person's only means of expressing needs or communicating distress.

Handout 6.2 Key risk factors for suicide

While self-harm is not to be confused with suicide, an assessment of the risk of death or serious injury is essential for clients with a history of injuring themselves. In this context we are looking at the risk of the person dying or sustaining a serious injury by self-inflicted means irrespective of whether the end result is accidental or intentional.

While there exists no reliable tool to assess the risk of death or serious injury, the following is a list of factors that are closely linked with suicide and, given the circumstances in which the assessment is taking place, may offer useful pointers in suggesting safe management, or determining a more thorough assessment and possible referral to a general practitioner or more specialist mental health input:

- low mood

- feelings of hopelessness

- an inability to look toward the future

- history of depression, schizophrenia or other severe mental illness

- physical illness or disability

- heavy use of drugs and/or alcohol

- a history of past suicide attempts

- clear plans (changes to financial details, wills etc.)

- a past record of violence to others.

✓

Pandora's box

Much as care staff should aim towards establishing a strong rapport and a trusting relationship with the self-harming client, one-to-one work can reveal long-suppressed emotions and thoughts. Workers should be prepared for a possible short-term increase in severity and frequency of self-harm as these emotions come to the surface, often for the first time. It is advisable for staff to make use of professional supervision and the advice of colleagues in these situations, and to make referrals to a GP or community mental health team if appropriate.

Self-awareness

Discussing self-harm and suicide can be a very unpleasant experience. Care staff may have to confront deeply held beliefs and even antagonism toward those who choose to injure themselves in this way. Again, appropriate use of supervision and the advice of colleagues will prove invaluable, particularly where staff are left feeling distressed and uncomfortable working with a person who sets out to deliberately injure and disfigure themselves.

Seeking help

If a mental health or housing worker can offer a non-judgemental and empathetic response to a self-harming client, this may well be a 'lifetime first' for that individual. However, even within the best helping relationships more specialist intervention may be required. A GP will be able to make a referral to either a community mental health team or, in many cases, a qualified counsellor attached to the primary health care team. See also the list of resources and support groups earlier in this chapter.

Emergency treatment

Many of those working with self-harming clients will have little in the way of medical qualifications and experience, and will need to seek help and advice where clients have injured themselves, particularly where a person is not well known to an agency. Even in cases where the client is well known, professional advice should be sought immediately if injuries become more frequent or severe than usual. Cases of overdose cannot be assessed visibly, and in situations where clients have reported having taken an overdose of either prescribed or 'over-the-counter' medication, medical advice should again be sought as soon as possible.

Self-harm

- the deliberate injury to body tissue without the intention to kill oneself

- approximately 150,000 A&E episodes every year in the UK

- lifetime incidence: male 2 per cent; female 3 per cent

- growing incidence among adolescents

- not a mental disorder, but may or may not be associated with mental health problems.

Suicide and self-harm: very different phenomena

- suicide: usually a planned act

- self-harm: often impulsive and 'mood driven'

- suicide: intention to end life

- self-harm: a means of survival

- suicide: predominantly male

- self-harm: predominantly female.

✓

Why do people harm themselves?

- taking control

- releasing tension

- communication

- negative body image

- stimulation

- mental disorder.

Helping people who self-harm

- no well-researched evidence for effectiveness of specific treatments

- some evidence for effectiveness of dialectical behaviour therapy (DBT)

- professional responses often negative and judgemental

- key questions:

  - Does self-harm actually present a problem for that person?

  - Are they clear that they wish to work on changing their behaviour, or trying to identify underlying factors?

Conclusion

As trainers in mental health care, we always like participants to leave a course with at least one 'golden nugget'. That is, one key piece of information, or a skill, or a 'Toolkit' item that will inform and improve their practice, and stay with them for many years. It is hoped this book, or the training courses and sessions that will be based on it, will also leave more than one 'golden nugget' in its wake, and we end with an attempt to briefly summarize and conclude those issues that really make a difference in community mental health care.

First, we set out to write a book that was as useful as possible to the widest range of practitioners, trainers and managers in a range of care settings. We have tried to keep a very firm focus on demystifying mental health problems. Myths and stereotypes have been clarified, and in a field of work which surely presents one of the greatest intellectual challenges of any job, we have tried to translate some very complex issues into plain English so that readers can make better sense of some of the problems presented by their clients. We have also tried to emphasize that, despite the undeniable importance of training and professional qualifications, the most crucial aspect of effective mental health care is the ability of practitioners to empathize, to show positive, optimistic attitudes, and to communicate effectively. This may appear a bold and sweeping statement and yet is based on our experience of talking to hundreds of people with mental health problems over the years. If the reader is left with an overriding sense of the importance of 'people skills' in mental health care, then we can feel we have done our job at least reasonably effectively!

Second, mental health workers will always be faced with people and situations which prove difficult and even impossible to manage, leaving all but the most resourceful and optimistic workers feeling dispirited, burnt out and 'de-skilled'. One common pitfall (especially for less experienced workers) is the impression that one hugely caring, talented and intelligent practitioner can single-handedly 'cure' a severely troubled person. This is the stuff of Tom Hanks, Robin Williams and Hollywood, not of supported housing or the local community mental health team, and it is unsurprising that workers are sometimes disappointed by the way their best efforts are rejected or even despised by their clients. We hope that this book has offered some inspiration, some fresh ideas, and has emphasized the fact that good community care is not necessarily based on the individual skills/brilliance/dedication of the keyworker or care co-ordinator, but on collaboration with the client, colleagues and other agencies and professionals. Nonetheless, there are many examples here of how even individual workers can make a huge difference to the lives of those with whom we work.

Third, while there is not a chapter entitled 'the importance of holistic care' in this book, we hope that the book has emphasized the truly multi-faceted nature of mental health and all its associated disorders, illnesses and social problems. Individuals may experience a multitude of problems which are not clearly defined and parcelled away in neat boxes with a sticky label saying 'schizophrenia' or 'personality disorder'. We may not have to look very far beyond dual diagnosis as an example of the complexity of issues that might be thrown up by just one individual, but even readers with little or no experience of mental health work may be surprised by the all-encompassing nature of mental health, and the equally all-encompassing care that is required to work successfully with very vulnerable people.

Causes of mental disorder (or 'aetiology') are equally diverse, although there is not necessarily any visible 'cause' at all. We have outlined the roles of neurotransmitters such as serotonin and dopamine in the progress of depression and schizophrenia, but would require a much weightier tome to describe in more detail the more complex social and psychological issues that both precede and catalyse mental health problems, and which play such an important role in both understanding and helping people with mental health problems.

And finally

Sadly, there are no 'magic bullets' or instant cures for the mental health problems we have discussed in this book, but if we have at least offered some understanding, raised awareness, and offered some valuable advice on how to work with mentally disordered people, then all the hard work will have been worthwhile!

Of course no amount of reading or even attending courses can compensate for what we learn through day-to-day work 'in the field', and we are confident that readers will be able to make a great deal more sense out of what are sometimes baffling situations, and are left better prepared to meet the needs of those people on the receiving end of our care and support. Good mental health care does not require a university degree, but does demand a high degree of compassion, common sense and the ability to think creatively. Above all, this is what this book has been about, and we hope it has helped you the reader realize the positive attitudes and wide range of skills you probably already had, but didn't have the time to realize!

Introducing the Mental Health Act 1983

Each year in England approximately 26,000 people are admitted to psychiatric care under the auspices of the Mental Health Act (MHA) 1983, with a further 18,000 being 'detained' or 'sectioned' following informal or voluntary admission (Department of Health 2003). It is a common misconception that the MHA exists for the sole purpose of 'locking people up'. However, the MHA is far more complex and wide-ranging than this, encompassing guidance and legislation on many aspects of care, the rights of patients and their families, and the responsibilities of professionals. The MHA provides the legal framework that not only protects the rights of patients, but also professionals and the public. It is also important to remember that the legal powers outlined here apply to clearly designated settings such as hospitals and statutory services, and in almost all circumstances cannot be enforced in community settings such as patients' homes, group homes or supported accommodation.

The MHA is divided into ten 'parts' and has 149 'sections', each of which is divided into sub-sections. This appendix will refer only to the most commonly used sections, and those that readers are most likely to see referred to in reports and correspondence.

A glossary of terms used in the Mental Health Act

An understanding of these terms is helpful in working with and supporting those individuals who have been subject to the Act. The MHA has its own terminology referring to very specific legal meanings and powers. Some of these terms may be quite familiar although their exact meaning may be unclear.

Section 12 doctor

A 'Section 12 doctor' is a doctor who has 'special experience in the diagnosis of treatment of mental disorder'. In practice, he or she will normally be a senior psychiatrist and is government-approved to make recommendations for the compulsory detention of the mentally ill. Most mental health units have a rota of approved Section 12 doctors providing 24-hour availability. Most of the MHA's powers to detain require at least one recommendation from a Section 12 doctor.

Approved social worker (ASW)

An approved social worker (ASW) is a social worker who has undergone specialist training in mental health and mental health law and has experience of working with the mentally ill or learning disabled. The Act states that they must have 'appropriate competence in dealing with persons who are suffering from mental disorder'.

ASWs are employed by the local authority and are effectively independent of the health service. It is the ASW that makes an application for compulsory detention, having been satisfied that the legal grounds for detention have been met, that the person is suffering from a mental disorder as specified in the Act, and that a safe alternative to hospital admission is not available.

Before making an application, the ASW will have conducted a thorough assessment and consulted with the patient's 'nearest relative' (see below) and, where possible, professionals who know the individual. In addition, the ASW is responsible for the safe transportation of the patient to hospital. Their role is described as a statutory role (defined by law) and cannot be delegated. Local authorities provide a rota of ASWs to ensure 24-hour availability. Following the assessment, the ASW has to provide a report outlining why the assessment was necessary and their reasons for detaining or not detaining the patient. In addition to their role of making the application for detention, the ASW also has statutory duties to provide reports for and attend a mental health review tribunal (MHRT).

Mental health review tribunal

Within time periods specified by the MHA, detained patients and their nearest relatives have the right to appeal to the mental health review tribunal against further detention. With the power to discharge detained patients, the tribunal is a formal legal hearing and the patient has the right to request legal representation. The tribunal panel is appointed by the Lord Chancellor and consists of a lawyer, a medical member and a lay person.

Responsible medical officer (RMO)

The responsible medical officer (RMO) is the doctor in charge of the detained patient's treatment, usually the patient's consultant psychiatrist. A patient has only one RMO, who has clearly designated powers that only they can perform. If the RMO is going to be absent for any period of time he or she must delegate responsibility to another senior doctor in their absence.

Section 17 – planned and authorized leave from hospital

As part of a patient's treatment and discharge planning, the multi-disciplinary team must assess how the patient will readjust to normal life in the community. This assessment is made by the patient having periods of leave from hospital, and can only be authorized by the RMO under Section 17 of the MHA. When granting Section 17 leave the RMO must specify: whether the leave is for a fixed or indefinite period; whether the patient needs to be escorted on leave by a member of hospital staff; or whether any conditions need to be attached to the leave. For example, in the case of overnight leave the patient must sleep at a certain address. The RMO can also extend a patient's leave or revoke the leave at any time if it is in the interests of the patient's safety or for the protection of others.

Section 117 – after-care

Under Section 117, health trusts and social services have to provide after-care to patients who have been detained and treated under the Mental Health Act. Section 117 responsibilities continue even after the patient has been discharged from the section that detained them in hospital.

All patients receiving specialist mental health services must be registered under the care programme approach (CPA) (see Chapter 2 Treatment and Support) and be assigned a 'care coordinator'. When patients are discharged from hospital the care plan must specify the required after-care arrangements. For patients who are subject to Section 117, the care plan has to be agreed by the relevant statutory services. Through Section 117 arrangements, funding can be requested to enable the delivery of care (such as appropriate accommodations, work retraining or further education) identified in the care plan.

The Mental Health Act: Part I

Part I of the Act provides legal definitions of mental disorder, which it describes thus: 'Mental illness, arrested or incomplete development of mind, psychopathic disorder and any other disorder or disability of mind.' The Mental Health Act then describes four categories of mental disorder, the criteria for which must be met before compulsory admission can be considered. For the detention to be lawful the section papers signed by a doctor(s) have to specify which disorder the patient is suffering from to be within the scope of the Act. The categories are as follows.

Severe mental impairment

'A state of arrested or incomplete development of mind which includes severe impairment of intelligence and social functioning and is associated with abnormally aggressive or seriously irresponsible conduct on the part of the person concerned.'

Mental impairment

'A state of arrested or incomplete development of mind (not amounting to severe mental impairment) which includes significant impairment of intelligence and social functioning and is associated with abnormally aggressive or seriously irresponsible conduct on the part of the person concerned.'

Psychopathic disorder

'A persistent disorder or disability of mind (whether or not including significant impairment of intelligence) which results in abnormally aggressive or seriously irresponsible conduct on the part of the person concerned.'

Mental illness

Mental illness is by far the most frequent basis for detention. The MHA does not define mental illness, but allows doctors to apply strictly clinical (as opposed to legal) criteria in determining whether an individual is mentally ill. For example, schizophrenia is a clinical (as opposed to legal) diagnosis, but is a form of mental illness as defined by the

Act. However, two doctors must agree that a person is mentally ill before a section can be applied.

The Mental Health Act: Part II

Part II is concerned with hospital admissions and guardianship, and describes the more familiar sections (often referred to as the 'civil sections') of the Act under which 90 per cent of detained patients are admitted (Department of Health 2003). Part II of the Act allows a patient to be compulsorily admitted under the Act where this is necessary:

- in the interests of his/her own health

- in the interests of his/her own safety

- for the protection of other people.

Table A.1 outlines the most commonly used admission sections under Part II of the Mental Health Act 1983.

The Mental Health Act: Part III

Part III of the MHA applies to prisoners or those involved in criminal proceedings, and can apply to remand and sentence prisoners. Table A.2 gives a brief explanation of the most commonly used sections for this patient group, although there are several more that have not been included as they are generally applied in specialist settings such as secure units and special hospitals and are beyond the remit of this book.

Reference

Department of Health (2003) *Department of Health Statistical Bulletin (2003/22): In-patients Formally Detained in Hospitals Under the Mental Health Act 1983 and Other Legislation, England: 1992–93 to 2002–2003.* London: The Stationery Office.

Useful resources

Websites

HyperGUIDE to the Mental Health Act: www.hyperguide.co.uk/mha

Mind: The Mental Health Act 1983, an outline guide: www.mind.org.uk/Information/Legal/OGMHA.htm

The Institute of Mental Health Act Practitioners: www.markwalton.net

Book

Jones, R. (2001) *Mental Health Act Manual.* London: Sweet & Maxwell.

Table A.1 Part II of the Mental Health Act: key sections

Section	Purpose	Requirements	Grounds for Detention	Duration
2	Admission for assessment	An application based on two medical recommendations, one of whom must be a Section 12 doctor	The patient must be suffering from a mental disorder of a nature and degree that requires the patient to be detained in hospital in the interests of his/her own safety or for the protection of the general public	28 days
3	Treatment	An application and two medical recommendations, one of which must be made by a Section 12 doctor. If possible one doctor must have had previous acquaintance of the patient	That the patient is suffering from a mental disorder as defined in the Mental Health Act. In addition the disorder must be of a nature or degree that requires the patient to be detained in hospital in the interest of his/her safety or for the protection of the public. In the case of psychopathic disorder or mental impairment there is a further condition that a treatment is likely to 'alleviate or prevent a deterioration of the condition'	Initially six months. If further detention is required the section can be renewed initially for six months then annually up to one year
4	Emergency admission for assessment	One application based on one medical recommendation made by either a doctor who knows the patient or a Section 12 doctor	For extreme emergencies where a patient's condition warrants immediate admission and there is insufficient time to arrange a second medical recommendation that would cause 'undesirable delay'. The reason for using Section 4 must be clearly stated	72 hours
5(2)	Doctor's holding power	A doctor who is the patient's doctor or nominated deputy. The doctor must provide the hospital managers with a report justifying the reason for detention	For the legal detention of a patient who wants to leave hospital but is assessed as not well enough to do so	72 hours – this is considered sufficient time to assess the patient and for an application for Section 2 or 3 to be made. The section expires at the end of 72 hours
5(4)	Nurse's holding power	A first-level nurse (RMN). The nurse must record in writing the conditions for the detention and provide the hospital managers with a report as to why detention was necessary	To prevent an informal patient from leaving the ward if there is evidence that the patient is suffering from a mental disorder and detention is necessary for the patient's safety or the safety of the public. Only to be used if it is not possible for a doctor to immediately attend the ward	Six hours, during which time the patient must be examined by a doctor. The detention ends when the doctor arrives on the ward. The time Section 5(4) was applied must be noted because if the doctor decides to apply Section 5(4) the 72 hours starts from when Section 5(4) was applied

Table A.2 Part III of the Mental Health Act: key sections

Section	Purpose	Requirements	Grounds for Detention	Duration and Rights
37	Enables the court to send an offender to hospital for treatment	Can be imposed at either the Magistrates or Crown Court. In the case of the Magistrates Court the court only has to be satisfied that the offender committed the offence for which they are accused. In the Crown Court the offender has to be convicted. The hospital has to agree to admit the patient within 28 days	The court must be satisfied on the evidence of two doctors, one of whom is Section 12 approved, that the offender is suffering from a mental disorder as defined in the Act	Initially six months. Can be renewed for a further six months and then annually. During the first six months neither the patient nor their nearest relative have a right to appeal to the MHRT
41	A restriction order can only be applied to Section 37. It is not a stand-alone section	Only the Crown Court can apply a restriction order once a person has been convicted of an offence punishable by imprisonment. A Magistrates Court can refer a case to the Crown Court for a restriction order to be applied. The RMO has to agree to provide the Home Office with reports of the patient's progress at least once a year. The patient cannot leave hospital without the permission of the Home Office	As for Section 37 plus: the court must take into consideration the nature of the offence; the person's criminal history; the risk of the person committing further offences; protecting the public from serious harm	With or without limit of time. The patient can apply to an MHRT between six and 12 months of the order being made, and then every subsequent 12 months. The Home Office must approve all periods of leave based on the current risk assessment
47	Transfer to hospital of sentenced prisoners	Transfer has to take place within 14 days of the order being made	The criteria is the same as for sections under Part II of the Act and Section 37 with the added criteria that the Home Office is of the opinion that transfer is necessary having first considered the interests of the public	No limit of time. Transfer comes to an end on the earliest date that the patient could have been released from prison if they had not been transferred to hospital. However, if the person still requires detention after this date they automatically become reclassified as a 'notional Section 37'
49	A restriction order that the Home Office can apply to Section 47	Can be imposed by the Home Secretary where further restriction of the prisoner is deemed necessary	The criteria for special restrictions on transferred prisoners are similar to those for 5.41 (above)	No limit of time. If the patient no longer requires hospital treatment the Home Office has to be informed so that the patient can be returned to prison

Subject Index

Author Index